CW00617638

EXPRESS COMMUNITY

EXPRESS COMMUNITY:

BRINGING SOCIAL ACTION TO LIFE:

A RESOURCE-FULL GUIDE FOR GROUP LEADERS

Phil Bowyer

Copyright © 2004 Phil Bowyer

10 09 08 07 06 05 04   7 6 5 4 3 2 1

First published 2004 by Spring Harvest Publishing Division and Authentic Media
9 Holdom Avenue, Bletchley, Milton Keynes, Bucks, MK1 1QR, UK
and PO Box 1047, Waynesboro, GA 30830-2047, USA.
www.authenticmedia.co.uk

The right of Phil Bowyer to be identified as the author
of this work has been asserted by him in accordance
with the Copyright, Designs and Patents Act 1988.

All rights reserved.

All rights reserved. No part of this publication may be reproduced,
stored in a retrieval system, or transmitted in any form or by any means,
electronic or mechanical, including photocopy, recording or otherwise,
without the prior permission of the publisher or a licence permitting restricted
copying. In the UK such licences are issued by the Copyright Licensing Agency,
90 Tottenham Court Road, London W1P 9HE.

Unless otherwise indicated, all Scriptural quotations are from
the HOLY BIBLE, NEW INTERNATIONAL VERSION
© 1973, 1978, 1984 by the International Bible Society.
Used by permission of Hodder & Stoughton, a member of Hodder Headline Ltd.
All rights reserved.

British Library Cataloguing in Publication Data.
A catalogue record for this book is available from the British Library.

ISBN 1-85078-583-X

Cover design by 4-9-0 ltd
Illustrations by Matt Lomax
Typeset by Temple Design
Print Management by Adare Carwin

CONTENTS

BEST SUPPORTING ROLES

Rachel and Zach – my best example of community!

For the security of belonging, the strength of believing and the stacks of blessing you continually bring into my life – thank you!

'Though one may be overpowered, two can defend themselves. A cord of three strands is not quickly broken' (Ecc. 4:12).

FOREWORD

If we as Christians desire to engage with the world that God so loves then two things need to happen. First we need to capture God's heart for this world and our communities, and secondly we need to act. Phil Bowyer's fantastic book, *Express Community*, challenges us to do both. It highlights the need to understand our calling to be good news in our communities, and provides the tools necessary to fulfil that calling.

As we read through the gospels we cannot help but notice that as Jesus walked upon the earth with his 12 disciples, there was a mighty proclamation of the good news and the kingdom of heaven, and with it came a powerful demonstration of what that kingdom was like. This ministry of proclamation and demonstration continued in the early church. Demonstration of the kingdom came in the form of signs and wonders, as Jesus promised, and also in the inclusive, open-hearted community of the believers. The believers were known for their extravagant generosity in sharing their possessions with the poor, accepting orphans and widows into their community, and caring for the broken and sick. In that context, people were desperate to hear what the early church had to say. It is no surprise that the Lord 'added to their number daily those who were being saved'.

The early believers did not live in this radical way because it was evangelistically effective. They lived in this way because of worship. They had been called to such a life and gave their whole beings as their worship to the Almighty. If the motivation had been evangelism I think they would have hit burn-out, but the motivation was simply worship, and out of the overflow of worship comes evangelism. The early believers were radical worshippers first and foremost, and then became known as radical evangelists. Wouldn't it be amazing if we saw growth like they saw today in our churches and youth groups? Why don't we?

I recently read the following words from Jim Wallis in his book *The Call to Conversion*:

> The evangelism of the church has no power when the essence of the gospel is not lived out ... When the life of the church no longer raises any questions, evangelism degenerates.

As I read these words they hit me, and have been with me ever since. Maybe they are truer today than ever before. Young people are not always the greatest listeners, at least when you want them to listen, but they are fantastic watchers. It is almost as if they have been trained through the endless reality TV shows to watch from a distance and come to their own conclusions on individuals and groups. They are more than able to sniff out hypocrisy and spot the genuine article. That might make youth work sound terrifying, but it provides an amazing opportunity for young people to be impacted through the gospel being lived out in our lives and in the lives of other young people around them. You can only watch with intrigue for a certain amount of time before the questions start to flow, and then we need to be ready to answer (note 1 Peter 3:15). Will they listen? People always listen to the answers of the questions they have asked!

The assumption is that the gospel is lived out, not just in our Christian communities, but also in all of the communities to which we belong. For those searching to discover what that might mean and look like, *Express Community* is a brilliantly practical guide and tool for groups of young people, students and young adults. Phil includes insights into what the Bible has to say about communities and our roles within them, some incredibly helpful thoughts on how to connect with your community and identify the needs within it, and lots of creative thinking on how we can get involved and practically, and in a meaningful way, demonstrate God's love to our communities.

This book is full of gems and, if acted upon, could be the source of effective discipleship to people in the church, effective outreach to people outside the church, and a means of building bridges between the two. I thoroughly recommend Phil as a writer whom I respect and admire, and his *Express Community* as an excellent resource.

Pete Hughes
Associate Director
Soul Survivor UK

PREFACE

Express Community is designed to encourage, enable and equip youth, student and young adult groups to become more involved with their community. *Express Community* aims to enable people to become an integral part of what goes on in a specific location. It is an attempt to avoid the trap, which some community work falls into, of Christians 'doing to' or 'acting on behalf of' a community rather than 'living within'. As a result of completing the process, groups may decide to start a specific initiative to meet a need highlighted by implementing the procedure suggested by the guide; they may choose to join and support existing initiatives of which they have become aware; or alternatively they may feel that for now they have been challenged to make some simple changes to their lifestyle that enable them more effectively to 'express community'.

The philosophy of and some of the inspiration for this book originates from Tearfund's *Church, Community and Change* manual, written by Tulo Raistrick. Tearfund is an evangelical Christian relief and development charity working through local partners to bring help and hope to communities in need around the world. The purpose of Tearfund is to serve Jesus Christ by enabling those who share evangelical Christian beliefs to bring good news to people living in poverty. *Church, Community and Change* has been used to help Tearfund partners across the UK and Ireland to respond to their community appropriately.

Express Community draws on the experience of *Church, Community and Change*, Tearfund's UK and Ireland team, and that of many other evangelical Christians who have chosen to develop an integral view of life that sees living within community as their mission and calling. Our prayers and appreciation go out to them all.

OPENING CREDITS

There are so many people to whom I will be eternally grateful for their contributions towards this book. It seems unfair to single out a few. However, I would like to say how particularly grateful I am to Dewi Hughes, Jim Hartley and Rachel Bowyer. Your willingness to sit, sift and critique masses of material in order to get this book to where it is today has already blessed me, and will bless others who read and use it. Your sacrificial support, creative concern and sensitive suggestions, plus your willingness to go that extra mile(s!) to ensure this book was the best it could be continue to astound me.

I would also like to thank friends and colleagues who, as well as being influential in shaping the purpose of this resource, have added specific content and ideas: Lorna Duddy, Zoe Hayes, Andy Baldwin, David Westlake and Nigel Roberts. Thank you for all your comments on numerous drafts. Thanks in this regard are also due to Patrick Parkes, Geoff Harley Mason and Pete Hughes for their input and contributions.

And finally, my thanks go to those who contributed in ways they will never realise: to Mick Ellor, for believing and investing in me; to Pete Read, for your model of leadership – as teacher, at church and within family; and to Gordon Thomas, for inspiring me to read and preach God's word.

Thanks also to Matt Lomax for the creative way you have chosen to illustrate this resource and for your valuable friendship.

This really is a book for community, by community.

Thank you.

Phil Bowyer
March 2004

SETTING THE SCENE

BRINGING SOCIAL ACTION TO LIFE

'Love the Lord your God with all your heart and with all your soul and with all your mind and with all your strength.' The second is this: 'Love your neighbour as yourself.' There is no commandment greater than these (Mk. 12:30-31).

Thriller or romantic comedy, action or romance, social action or evangelism? It's a simple question that cannot be ignored when you're deciding genre, particularly in a book called *Express Community*. Ratings suggest that if you're looking for a box office hit, it's hard to beat a thrilling all-action romantic comedy. Seriously, no book on community would be complete without addressing the social action versus evangelism question. It may be an age-old debate but I feel it's one that deserves some attention right at the start of this process. Let's deal with it now, deciding the general theme, before we even think about explaining what might happen as part of the main feature.

CHOICES TO BRING *OUR* MISSION TO LIFE

So which is it to be: social action or evangelism, or can it be both? According to popular opinion it certainly seems it can be both, with titles like Social Evangelism, Action Evangelism or Integral Mission showing more regularly than in previous years. In an ideal world there should be room for both and, let's face it, it *is* an ideal world that God's after! The extent to which you are successful in giving equal screen-time to both social action and evangelism will depend on your motivation for getting involved in your community in the first place. As you begin to consider how to 'express community', you may find it helpful to pause for a moment and ask yourself whether as a group of Christians you are concerned for community because a) you know God wants you to care about people, or b) you care about people knowing God.

We could spend the whole introduction discussing the most appropriate words or phrases to describe what we intend to do in our community, but quite frankly who cares? Your community certainly doesn't. What matters to them is how real, relevant and reliable your relationships with them are. When they sit down to view the premiere of your ideas about what a better community might look like, the questions at the forefront of their minds will be who's starring in it, whether it's any good, whether it's going to be any different from anything else they've seen, or whether they have seen it all before. Is this going to be just another one of those scripts that promise a lot but in the end have no plot? Like any good home movie, whilst the cover may grab you, you'll be less concerned with the title and more with what it's about and how it leaves you feeling afterwards.

JESUS BRINGS GOD'S *CO*-MISSION TO LIFE

Any critique on the role of mission has to start with the obvious question – how did Jesus choose to play it? If you look at the mission of Jesus, it seems he sees both action and evangelism as playing an equally significant role. Jesus didn't seem to distinguish between the two – his mission involved both. How he lived that out is something we'll explore in more depth in Chapter 1. For now, a brief read of Jesus' script and it's quite clear that social action and evangelism get equal screen-time.

The great commission of Matthew 28:18-20 is often used to explain the concept of mission. Read it and it's easy to see why in many missions, social action plays the supporting role to evangelism's lead. Jesus opens with a line that calls his disciples to make disciples of others and closes with the reassurance that he will be with them as they do so. But is there more to it than that? Any young person who ever paid attention at school will tell you that all good stories should have a middle as well as a beginning and an end. Rewind, pause and replay the beginning of verse 20. Jesus' commission does not stop at simply finding people, baptising people and stopping only long enough to hang them out to dry, before quickly moving on. As well as the 'going', an integral part of the great commission involves 'making'. How? Jesus says, by 'teaching them to obey everything I have commanded you'. So at the heart of the great commission is commandment.

So what does Jesus command? A quick search through his life will throw up reels of commands, but skip back a few scenes to Matthew 22:34-40 or Mark 12:29-31 and you'll find what Jesus considers to be the greatest. Here Jesus chooses a combination of two commandments, loving God and loving others, to answer a question about which is 'the greatest'. Is this enough to stamp out the evangelism/social action debate in your mind? Or do you feel this only stirs things up further? Look again. The answer to *our* question is not found in the answer but in the question. Although Jesus' answer is indeed plural, the question is thoroughly singular: '... which is *the* greatest?' (Mt. 22:36) is the original query and in return Jesus replies:

a) 'Love the Lord your God with all your heart and with all your soul and with all your mind and with all your strength.'

b) 'Love your neighbour as yourself.'

Even under pressure to choose between the two, it seems that Jesus is not prepared to cut one for the sake of the other (see also Mk. 12:29-31). The teacher of the law asked 'which is the greatest?', but Jesus responds with a both/and answer. If Jesus cannot split them, how can we? Jesus' answer combines two essential elements that form one integral whole. It seems evangelism and social action *both* play leading roles in the greatest commandment, and therefore it seems safe to say that this is the case with the great commission also. The challenge we face is how to get the balance right!

Since evangelism is essentially concerned with how people come to know and love God, it would seem it takes care of the first half of Jesus' greatest command. If we choose to live according to God's holy 'co-mission', then like that of Jesus, our mission should begin to address people's need to hear and experience the good news that Jesus loves sinners and died in order to save them. Responding to this will

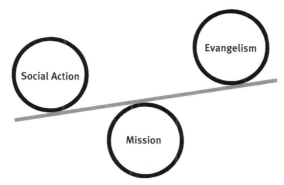

give them a better life now and forever. The weakness of some evangelism is that as people focus on saving souls for heaven they miss the fact that it is as much about saving situations on earth. Jesus' mission was never simply to love and save souls. His mission was to meet and minister to a people he loved. Though he was fully God, he was also fully human, someone who ate, slept and wept alongside other human beings (Mt. 21:18; Mt. 8:24; Jn. 11:35). He loved people and because of this he wanted to give them opportunities to experience a life that was 'more abundant' than ever (Lk. 6:38). As people commit to Christ, their renewed sense of value, worth and purpose – as a direct consequence of his love – frequently raises their level of self-confidence. As a result of this new-found faith in God and themselves they soon begin to access opportunities that they once considered impossible and out of reach.

A mission focused on challenging people to love God will create change in their lives if they choose to see their need for him and respond accordingly. However, it is important to recognise that any individual's ability to see his or her need to love God starts by others first loving them and ends with them loving others. Again this is something we'll consider more in Chapter 1. In the meantime, ask yourself this: if Jesus loved people, not just 'souls', shouldn't we? No matter how long you spend 'connecting within community', you'll never meet 'souls', just people: people created in God's image whom God, as a consequence of living under his authority, would love to see living better lives amongst their families, friends and the wider community. It is through social action that people generally begin to find ways to love each other in the way the great commandment demands. Action provides opportunities for people to have relationship with others, which, should they respond, will impact their view of the past, their picture of the present and their role in the future. How people respond to social action may or may not include God, but it will involve some degree of change – again a concept we'll explore more in Jesus' model of integral mission in Chapter 1.

JESUS BRINGS GOD'S *INTEGRAL* MISSION TO LIFE

In an attempt to wrap up this debate then, it seems that as a result of this short critique, neither evangelism nor social action should feel like an optional extra. We know that our relationship with God is the most important of all and that messing up there is the reason why we mess up in all the others. If somehow we could get our relationship with God straight, then straightening up relationships we have with others should become easier – he becomes Lord over *all* my life. The Micah Network, a worldwide group of more than 200 evangelical Christian relief, development and justice agencies, defines integral mission as follows:

> *Integral mission or holistic transformation is the proclamation and demonstration of the gospel. It is not simply that evangelism and social involvement are to be done alongside each other. Rather, in integral mission our proclamation has social consequences as we call people to love and repentance in all areas of their lives and our social involvement has evangelistic consequences as we bear witness to the transforming grace of Jesus Christ.*[1]

As a Christian you are by default a follower of Christ. In the great commandment and the great commission, Jesus sees loving God and loving others as interlocking elements of a life built on discipleship. This then should be your aim for life.

JESUS BRINGS *HIS LIFE* TO GOD'S INTEGRAL MISSION

As if to show more clearly the strong relationship between social action and evangelism, Jesus, through the incarnation, offers his own life as a kind of filter, funnel or clarifying focus through which to view God's mission formula. As always, he turns things on their head and shows us that the way to a more balanced mission lies in looking at the *who*, rather than the *what* or *why*.

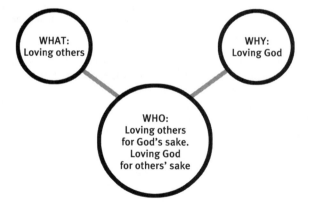

The focal point of *what* he did and *why* he did it was *who* he was – that's *how* he lived! Though Jesus' life may have included great acts of social concern alongside great acts of evangelism, their impact comes from who he was. At no point were Jesus' actions for the benefit of the camera; his was a life of integrity. As we seek to serve our communities we cannot turn our compassion on and off like a tap. We have to become fully committed, fully involved at every level of our life. Jesus' mission was his life and his life was his mission: it was hard to see where one stopped and the other started.

Throughout his life Jesus saw the importance of connecting with God in private and the effects this would have on his ability to care for the lives of the whole person in public. His integral commitment to God and to others was common to every aspect of his life and mission. As you consider what it means to express community through integral mission, being prepared to view *everything* you do under the one umbrella of a life which lives up to *who* God has called you to be, *what* he has called you to do and *why* he's chosen you to do it, will determine *how* easily you grasp hold of the vision he has for you, your group and your community.

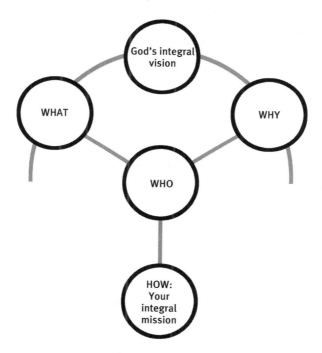

TOGETHER YOU CAN BRING INTEGRAL MISSION TO LIFE

Who you are will inevitably influence *what* you do and *why* you do it. Together all three will inform *how* you seek to live with others. God creates us in his image that we might declare his praises through a worship-full lifestyle of loving others. Worship that involves everything we say, do and are. Integral mission is all about relationships, simple day-in-day-out relationships, with God, with your group and with your community. *Express Community* is as much about addressing the need for change in your own life as it is about addressing the need in others. The Express Community process will help you to understand the *what* and *why* questions of mission in the context of a new understanding of *who* you, your group and your community are in God. This will in turn begin to inform *how* you begin to develop an integral mission within your community. At every stage, within every chapter, every section and every session of this process, you need to ask yourself these three simple questions. How you choose to reply will determine your next move, your next stop and ultimately your final destination. In Jesus, mission and lifestyle are inseparable – integral. If we are to be, like Jesus, effective in God's mission to his world, then just as he chose to live with integrity, so must we.

LEARNING FROM LIFE

After spending a considerable amount of time, money and energy getting to the cinema at Christmas, I was thoroughly disappointed to see my efforts were completely wasted on the film on view. A bad plot, bad acting, some apparently unnecessary bad language and a bad back were not helped by the fact that for the first hour the sound and the action were completely out of sync.

As we begin to consider how our lives measure up to the life of Jesus as part of the Express Community process, our actions should follow his words so that for the untrained observer it should be difficult to see where one ends and the other begins. Then, just maybe, we might see love all around us!

BRINGING INTEGRAL MISSION TO LIFE

Christianity is a faith about finding truth. You may be glad to hear that the truth, and in particular what this means for your community, is out there somewhere - the key to this process is whether you are prepared to go and find it. If you've chosen this book to add to your growing collection of quick-fix or self-help titles or 'manuals for dummies' which is already gathering dust on your shelves, then I'm afraid you may be disappointed. If you think it will give all the answers, it won't – though it is packed full of good material. If you think you can give it a quick read 30 minutes before you meet with your group, you can't. If you are reading this book simply because you think it would be another good topic for your group to cover, then don't. If you believe it might help you to think through issues you'll encounter within your community and what it means to be a Christian living within community, then it will. It's a model which builds on the collective experience of practitioners in the field of community development, the unique experiences of Christians throughout the UK and Ireland thoroughly involved in their communities and some of the personal successes and failures of trying to connect the faith I'm passionate about to the people with whom I share my life. However don't use this as an excuse not to engage your brain. It may be a good basis to start from, but like any model, it is not fool-proof, but rather a guide that will need to be contextualized in order to find a best fit for you, your group and your community.

In its simplest form *Express Community* is a guide to a process of looking at and learning from the life and mission of Jesus as a model of integral mission that you can follow within your community. If as a result you find that you are a Christian who simply finds ways of living within community that are more effective, then it has achieved its aims.

FOR WHOM, BY WHOM AND WITH WHOM?

Who you choose to use this resource with is pretty much down to you. It has been designed with youth, young adult or student groups in mind but could work equally well in cell or home groups. Your role as leader is key to the whole process. You are to act as facilitator to your group. Whilst you may feel it necessary to take control now and again, this process will only work if it is owned by both the group you lead and the community you live in. If you are part of a wider Christian community, such as a church or a CU, then *Express Community* will work best if it is run in the context of their mission to the community. We suggest some ideas about how you might go about this at the end of Chapter 1. The process will be most effective if the leadership to whom you are accountable are behind it. Communicate the overall vision of *Express Community* well, and they may even want to belong to it too.

STAGE BY STAGE

Express Community is designed to take you, your group and your community on a journey. We begin with Stage 1: Reflecting within Community, with what the Bible has to say and participants' feelings about the places they live and work. Stage 2: Connecting within Community focuses on connecting with the lives of the people with whom they meet. The process formally ends at Stage 3: Acting within Community and with the formulation of some kind of action, activity or lifestyle change that is appropriate to what it means as Christians to be living within community.

Throughout the book we offer reflections on 'express experience' – the example of others involved in community development training/practice; 'learning from life' – analogies from the everyday designed to help you think through the issues; 'biblical background' – explaining some of the context and ideas behind the theology; and finally some 'helpful hints' – simple guidance for your eyes only.

CHAPTER BY CHAPTER

Stage 1: Reflecting within Community is divided into two chapters: Chapter 1 begins by reflecting on the theology of community in the light of what Jesus has to say about the kingdom of God; Chapter 2 moves on to consider what the Bible has to say about the kind of lifestyle to which God might be calling us in response to the injustice that exists on our doorsteps.

Stage 2: Connecting within Community includes Chapter 3 on the need to look at our community in a different light and to acquire new skills and methods that will enable us to connect with our community needs more effectively. Chapter 4 highlights how, as well as listening, it is important to involve our community in identifying their own needs; it provides three simple steps to order your research, looking wider, stoping longer, and listening deeper.

Stage 3: Acting within Community draws the book towards some kind of conclusion by thinking about the value of developing a strategy. Chapter 5 considers what kind of vision, mission and aims are required in order to begin to provide solutions to the problems, suggesting intimacy with God as the way to discover this. Chapter 6 involves developing ideas to meet these solutions; it focuses on the need to work in partnership with your community to meet needs in the same way as when you identified those needs.

The Express Community process finishes by highlighting the need to keep going towards a conclusion, highlighting in particular how the need for continuing devotion and evaluation are key to the 'success' of however you decide to respond to the call to live within community.

SECTION BY SECTION

Each chapter is divided into sections specifically designed for your use, your group's use and your community's use. This is illustrated in the following way:

Explore yourself: background reading on the issues related to the theme for you as the group leader;

Engage your group: practical, easy-to-use session plans for you as leader to use with your group as together you go deeper into specific themes related to the issue;

Express together: how both you as leader and your group act on what you have learnt so far.

SESSION BY SESSION

The Engage your group section of each chapter includes three easy-to-use session plans. These are resources designed to engage your group in the issue you have just considered. There are 15 in all. The order we have suggested is what we consider to be the best way to progress through *Express Community*, however it is really up to you how you choose to do it. You may find you don't need to do every session; you may find you need some more than once. Whatever you decide, please be careful in your choice and pray about what is best for the process.

The structure of the whole looks like this:

Stage One: Reflecting within Community

1.	Belonging	When, where and why community happens
2.	Blessing	Understanding how to live for the sake of community
3.	Believing	How Christians are called to live in community
4.	Justice	God's call to day-to-day justice
5.	Mercy	God's understanding for those in need
6.	Humility	God's view on serving people

Stage Two: Connecting within Community

7.	Look	Steps to connect with community
8.	Stop	Skills to connect with community
9.	Listen	Methods to connect with community
10.	Look wider	The who, what and when of connecting
11.	Stop and go	Reviewing and identifying key issues
12.	Listen deeper	Checking conclusions

Stage Three: Acting within Community

13.	Issues	Reviewing the situation, planning a mission and establishing aims
14.	Ideas	Setting objectives, deciding tactics and action planning

The final scene: Living within Community

15.	Evaluation	The hits, misses and maybes so far

Each session includes various activities designed to engage your group; there should be enough there for most learning styles, ages and experience. Again do not feel you have to do them all, but choose with wisdom (more detailed guidelines on how to use the session plans can found on p. 11).

STEP BY STEP: JUST HOW LONG WILL ALL THIS TAKE?

Well, without sounding too ambiguous, it's hard to say: it all depends on you, your group and your community. Can you put a time on how long it will take to sit down and listen to someone talk about his or her community? All kinds of analogies relating to string and queries about its length come to mind, but that's not particularly helpful.

EXPRESS EXPERIENCE

After doing Chapter 3, session 9 once, the group I was leading felt God calling them to repeat it every week for a further six months!

There is no real time scale for completing Express Community. If I was a politician I might conclude that however long it takes will depend on however long it takes. The process described in this book could take you as little as 14 sessions to complete, not including the evaluation, which should be ongoing. However since we are talking about establishing a new way of living within community through establishing an integral mission, I advise you to take it steadier than that. It may help to see this book as something to consider *whilst* you get involved in your community, rather than something to do *before* you get involved in your community. Whilst it may be sensible to hold back from any major decisions until you have completed the book, there is no reason to wait until the penultimate chapter before you begin to use the new skills or ideas that hopefully you'll discover along the way. At every stage of this Express Community process there should be something that affects and impacts your life within community, whether it's something you read in the Bible, something you discuss as a group or something you discover about your community.

KEY QUESTIONS

1. *Who* do you want to lead through this process?
- an existing group
- a new group
- a number of leaders from different groups within your wider Christian community who will then do it with their groups?

2. *What* do you need to do next?
- Speak to the leader of the church/wider Christian community to which you belong to explain, expand upon and explore your reasons for starting this process.

3. *Why* are you doing this?
- Just another topic? – Think again!
- You are passionate about community. Are there others who may like to join you as you explore the issues surrounding local integral mission?
- You know others who are passionate about community.

4. Finally, *how* do you need to respond to what you have read so far?
- Promote: share your thoughts with others, contact people who you feel would benefit from this kind of process.
- Pray: alone and with other local leaders; perhaps consider raising some form of prayer support as you prepare and deliver some of the material.
- Pastoral support: do you need a mentor, coach or just someone to chat with to help to support you in your role as leader of this process?

BRINGING EXPRESS COMMUNITY TO LIFE

HOW TO USE THE SESSIONS EFFECTIVELY

What's involved?

Each session has several different elements. These include an activity to help get your group to think about the issue, a Bible passage to look at and discuss, and an opportunity at the end to reflect and pray about the issues that have been raised. The following logos tell you which are which parts:

Takeaway or lovingly prepared

The sessions need to be prepared in advance. You may need to collect some resources, so do not leave it all until 7.05pm the day your group is due to arrive at 8.00pm. No resource will work 'off the shelf' with every group. You are the expert on what sort of people will be there. Read the material and adapt it, as you know what will best suit, teach and challenge your group. Depending on how long you meet for, you may find you have more material than you need. Do not worry: this was a conscious decision on our part as we thought about the best way of compiling the resources. Better to have too much than too little. Be wise about how you choose what you keep and drop from each session. Ask yourself about the needs of your group, your community and how each individual activity may help or hinder your progress.

A guide knows the way

These sessions are hopefully going to challenge your group members. We all find changing our attitudes and behaviour difficult, especially when prompted by God. You need to have read the sessions and considered the issues yourself before you lead your group through them. The chapter segment called 'Explore yourself' will be especially important here. You may need to pray about your own attitudes when God prompts you to change. If this happens you will be in a strong position to help challenge the group.

Who changes these days anyway?

Express Community is all about changing attitudes and behaviour. So who exactly will change the way your group think? Our responsibility is to bring people into contact with God and his values. That is why we share our lives with others and teach them what God has said in the Bible. It is then the job of the Holy Spirit to convict people of their need to change. So do be confident,

- in God
- in the Bible
- in your material, which you have worked hard to prepare

Do not worry about:

- having to win the argument
- needing to see immediate results

Do remember to:

- pray for your group
- pray that God will convict people to change
- think of ways to help your group to do something about what they have learned; Express together will be particularly important here

Some extra tips for using these sessions successfully with your group

- Get feedback. If you want your group to shout out suggestions, first get them into a small group to think of them and ask them to appoint a spokesperson to do the feeding back. This saves them having to think and speak at the same time.
- Do further research. Before your session and once you have prepared, do some extra research. Try websites to get some extra and up-to-date information on the subject. Recap some of the key questions at the end of 'Explore yourself'.
- Use visuals. Think of some visuals that would be useful to set the scene. These could be pictures or objects that you could collect beforehand.
- Grill an expert. See if you can think of anyone, either in your group or wider community, who may have some first-hand knowledge or experience of the issues and invite him or her along.
- Have any equipment you need to hand. Always have the following to hand in case of emergency: A4 paper (and some larger sheets of paper too), some pens (including marker pens – and ones that work!), BluTac, a portable CD-player (appropriate music in the background can help to create a relaxed atmosphere). Try and use instrumental music as background to prayer.
- Draw on your own experience. Think about how you can bring your own experiences to what you are talking about.

---

[1] Cited in T. Chester, *Justice, Mercy and Humility: Integral mission and the poor* (Carlisle: Paternoster, 2002), pp. 2-3. The Micah Network was established in late-1999. Its aim is to meet the needs of the poor and oppressed through integral mission, and to encourage the wider church in its God-given responsibility to demonstrate God's love for the poor.

STAGE 1

REFLECTING WITHIN COMMUNITY

The kingdom of heaven is like a mustard seed, which a man took and planted in his field. Though it is the smallest of all your seeds, yet when it grows, it is the largest of garden plants and becomes a tree, so that the birds of the air come and perch in its branches (Mt. 13:31-32).

Chapter 1

THE NOW AND NOT QUITE YET

The resourcefulness of God's creation and in particular its constant struggle to survive at all costs is a nagging reminder that, whilst life may sometimes be difficult, God's handiwork can also be incredibly resilient. It seems that even in some of the most obscure and apparently infertile locations on earth, God's creativity still manages to find mechanisms for adapting creatures to their environment so they might grow. Forget polar ice caps or even hostile deserts, take time to reflect on your own back yard and you may find that life exists in some of the most unexpected places. Whilst contemplating this idea, my mind was drawn along this path as I began to question how the cress sitting in a damp bit of cotton wool was managing to grow on my window sill, how the moss on the garden wall was able to grow without soil, and how a daffodil at the end of our freshly laid tar macadam drive had the gall and the strength to struggle through to pierce the previously pristine surface. It seems that providing the right combination of essential elements exists in any given place, something supernatural is able to occur which makes life possible; recollection of GCSE biology tells me that for plants these would be water, sunlight and carbon dioxide. God takes these three things and processes them to give life – photosynthesis, if you're interested.[1] As long as these elements exist, it seems anything can survive almost anywhere. The more time you take to reflect on your community, in community with others, the more your view of the complexities of life will become extended. The more you stop to review, the more you'll ask why, and hopefully the more answers you'll find to questions about what people need in order to grow.

INTEGRAL MISSION IN COMMUNITY

Although some components of God's creation may have found ingenious ways to survive under some of the most extreme conditions, you may find that people are not always confident that they can. You'll discover this as you begin to connect with your community during Stage Two of the Express Community process: Connecting within Community. You may find that some people in your community are quite literally hanging on to life's limits by their fingertips. Far from thriving, they are barely surviving: as far as they are concerned they are hardly living. Each of us has a specific combination of essential needs: how you as a leader and your group choose to respond to those needs will determine how successful you are at bringing integral mission to life. Should an individual lack any one of the essential elements that creates, maintains and develops life, their ability to grow will be hampered. Integral mission, and *Express Community* as one way of discovering this, is concerned with discerning what these essential ingredients are. The fact that they may be different for almost everyone you meet is the real challenge. People do not grow just anywhere. It does not happen by chance; most of us need some form of care, support and encouragement in order to grow. You'll need godly guidance, a good grounding in the Bible and a little bit of get up and go.

Your role as leader throughout this whole Express Community process is particularly significant. Not only will you be aware of the need for your group to begin thinking about how to plant something of worth within your community, but you should also be aware of the need for your own thinking to grow and develop. Ensuring that you grow, your group grows and your community grows is a heck of a responsibility. Developing the Express Community process into something strong enough that whatever you choose to do as a result is big enough to stand the test of time will not be easy. That is why as part of this guide we have included opportunities for you to sit back and explore the issue by yourself as a foundation for the material we have prepared for your group. Before you even think about taking your group to the next level, this is *your* time to listen to God and reflect on your previous conclusions, God's convictions and any possible connections. It may just change your life. Part of the beauty of *Express Community* is that you are not expected to have all the know-how, all the energy or even all the ideas, just a willingness to be prepared to stand with others as you begin to take short simple steps in the right direction towards a better community. The question you will need constantly to ask yourself is where your feet need to go: in whose footsteps are you following and what imprint would you like to leave behind each time you move forward?

INTEGRAL MISSION IN THE KINGDOM

The kingdom of God was one of the key themes of Jesus' teaching and preaching. He regularly spoke of the kingdom of God, as did John the Baptist before him. Indeed, Jesus' first public words after his baptism and time of temptation in the wilderness were, 'Repent, for the kingdom of heaven is near' (Mt. 3:2). The kingdom of God is not so much a place, like the United Kingdom, but the rule of God in people's lives. This rule is expressed on earth through communities of disciples of Jesus Christ the King, who, in the power of the Holy Spirit, love each other and those that are outside their fellowship. Pause for a minute; ask yourself whether this sounds like a description of you and your group. The sessions throughout this stage should help to answer that question, or at least help you to understand what steps you and your group may need to take to head in this direction.

As we begin to 'express community', the extent to which we are prepared to live together as disciples in accordance with God's will is determined by how much we believe that Jesus is the king of our lives. To live together according to God's will is to express his kingdom here on earth. As people begin to commit to a relationship with the community that belongs to Jesus, i.e. your group or your wider church, they are in effect beginning to recognise that Jesus might well be someone worth having as king over their lives also. The kingdom of God is all about expressing community.

Since it is through experiencing the love of the Christian community that most people become Christians, it is vital that we express community towards those who do not yet belong. It starts with a group, church or community of believers who love Jesus and follow him, and who as a result are prepared to express this commitment as active love, a love that flows out to society at large. Whilst we recognise that we can neither establish nor extend the kingdom – God does that – we have an important role to play. God brings the kingdom; we pray, we read his word; and as we live in obedience to him with the help of his Spirit, he does the rest.

So what does Jesus' model of integral mission say to us as we work for the extension of God's kingdom in our community? What essential elements does he choose as he seeks to grow his kingdom?

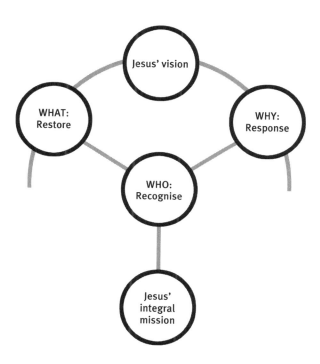

RECOGNISE: GOD SEEING PEOPLE'S NEEDS

In Matthew 9:35-38 we see Jesus faced with a crowd, but unlike us, he has the ability to see beyond the surface to the heart of the people's needs. Jesus sees them as harassed and helpless and because of that is filled with compassion for them. The word translated 'compassion' (v. 36) is a strong word. Seeing people as they are hits Jesus in the midriff. His is a gut reaction. It really hurts him to see people as they are. Do we see the people in need around us or do we choose to ignore them? And if we bother to look, how do we respond when we see people in need? Jesus sees a people who are 'harassed and helpless, like sheep without a shepherd'.

The phrase 'sheep without a shepherd' occurs a numbers of times in the Old Testament (e.g. Num. 27:17; 1 Kgs. 22:17), usually when Israel was in need of a ruler or leader. The job of rulers is to look after their people – to make sure that they are treated properly and that they have adequate food and shelter. In John 10:11 Jesus declares that he is the good shepherd, the ruler who will provide for and protect his people, and even die for them. Like sheep that have no shepherd, Jesus sees people as vulnerable to all sorts of evil. When Jesus sees people, he sees people not in control of their lives; they are sick, possessed and poor as a result of being pushed around by evil forces and powerful people. There is strong condemnation of those 'shepherds' who abandoned their people for their own ends in the Old Testament (see Ezek. 34). That Jesus has compassion on people because they have no shepherd suggests strongly that he also condemns those that do not care for them.

If we are honest, how often do we see people's needs? How often do we even look? The kingdom of God warmly welcomes those who are harassed and helpless. If we are to bring blessing into the lives of the people in our communities so that they may break free from the spiritual, social and economic forces that hold them captive, then we cannot do it alone. Noticing needs will take supernatural insight. Few workers share Jesus' compassion (Mt. 9:37) and without it the task ahead will be an impossible one. If we are to begin to see through the crowd to the reason for people's needs we are going to need godly recognition. Meeting those needs will require us to meet with God. Our relationship with him is just as crucial as his relationship with our communities.

RESTORE: GOD MEETING THE NEED OF PEOPLE

In Luke 4:18-19 Jesus' short but powerful attempt to replant a seed sown in the minds of Israel way back in the time of the prophets, which you will find in Isaiah 61:1-3 (and elsewhere), declares his arrival as God's new growth (see also Is. 11:1-5). Jesus makes it clear that he is the Messiah and the evidence of this will be seen in the transformation of the lives of the poor, outcast and marginalised.

> *The Spirit of the Lord is on me, because he has anointed me to preach good news to the poor. He has sent me to proclaim freedom for the prisoners and recovery of sight for the blind, to release the oppressed, to proclaim the year of the Lord's favour.*

Pretty much everyone is included in God's kingdom arrangements. The poor are at the forefront (Lk. 6:20), as are the marginalised and persecuted (Mt. 5:10), there's a new crop of Gentiles (Mt. 21:43), and even a bunch of sinners get a chance to blossom (Mk. 2:17). In fact, everyone gets a chance to feature (Col. 1:12-13). As you begin to follow Jesus in serving your community, you should expect to see positive outcomes for all types of people. Luke 4:18-19 is a wake-up call for Jesus' generation; his presence signifies that the promises of the past declared in Isaiah are becoming a reality in his life in the present.

In Matthew 4:12-13, 23-25 we see that Jesus initially went to where people were in order to do his work. It was as a result of his going out that people eventually came to him. His work mainly centres on teaching, preaching and healing. When teaching and preaching, he often used people's experience as a starting point (Mt. 9:16-17). He told many stories to communicate his message but also to make people think (Mt. 13:34). He also used everyday objects to make tangible connections between people's lives and his teaching (Mt. 6:26-29). Finally, rather than coming at people with all the answers he would ask questions in order to involve them in the process of meeting their needs (Mt. 6:25-28). Jesus' teaching tended to focus on spelling out the implications of the coming kingdom for the way people should behave. In our efforts to restore God's idea of community, we should not forget the value of both teaching and preaching. If used sensitively and relevantly they are extremely effective tools to enable people to meet their own needs. Let's face it, the Bible is packed full of good advice on how to live. However, though powerful, the Bible without action feels like a load of lifeless words to most of our communities: *Express Community* is designed to increase your ability to unlock this power through loving others and loving God. The problem for many within our community is that our words do not always measure up to the way we live our lives.

The thing that made Jesus' model of restoration distinct was that his works and wonders did measure up to his words. He lived out what he taught. The wonder of Jesus was that his 'miracles', literally his works, conveyed the same message as his words, as John 10:38 states: 'Even though you do not believe me, believe the miracles, that you may know and understand that the Father is in me, and I in the Father.'

Matthew records many of Jesus' miracles in his gospels. He shared the Jewish and scriptural belief that sickness is the result of living in a fallen world: if there were no sin there would be no sickness. That Jesus healed therefore was a sign that the tyranny of sin was retreating before the power of the kingdom of God. Jesus instantly frees people in all different categories – the demonised (Mk. 1:34), the diseased (Mt. 8:2-3), and even the dead (Lk. 7:14-15) – to show that the power of God's kingdom is at work in him.

The kingdom of God is about relieving suffering, recognising people's mental or physical pain and helping them to find a way out. It is not always about one-off grand actions. Focusing on the major miracles of Jesus can sometimes be a barrier to our willingness to express community. We might respond: 'We could *never* do that!' Often Jesus used everyday 'minor' miracles to bring about restoration in people's lives. Perhaps what your community really needs is someone actually to listen to them, someone to serve them, or for someone to be prepared to sacrifice something on their behalf. You *could* do that! Jesus' restoration ministry tells us a lot about the kingdom of God. Fixing, repairing, mending and healing all need to be evident in whatever daily action we choose to take in order to express community.

RESPONSE: PEOPLE SEEING THEIR NEED OF GOD

In the same way that it was Jesus' mission to bring God's heavenly kingdom to earth, it was just as much his mission to open the way to bring God's earth to his heavenly kingdom. The way people respond to Jesus determines both the course of their lives from that point onwards and also whether or not they will enter the eternal kingdom. The glory of the gospel is that God makes it possible for us to enter the kingdom by forgiving our past sins because of what Jesus did on the cross. To want forgiveness we must first realise that there are things in our lives that are wrong; we must want to get rid of those evil things. Repentance means responding to the challenge to turn away from sin, leaving it behind for good. When people meet God, through seeing the difference he makes to them personally, to situations known to them, or to how they think about a particular issue, and when they then decide to make a commitment, the Bible is clear that as well as expecting to see a difference in their lives here on earth (Lk. 19:1-10), they will also spend eternity with him (Lk. 23:42-3). Though people are called to live the life of eternity in the here and now, their experience of a kingdom community on earth will only be made complete as they see the full reality of Christ's heavenly kingdom on his return. Matthew 25:31-34 states: 'When the Son of Man comes in his glory, and all the angels with him, he will sit on his throne in heavenly glory. Then the King will say to those on his right, "Come, you who are blessed by my Father; take your inheritance, the kingdom prepared for you since the creation of the world."'

Despite what people saw Jesus say and do, they did not always respond to him in the same way: some join him and some leave him (see Lk. 5:1-11 and Jn. 6:60-70), and as far as we're made aware some stay the same, others choose to change their behaviour (see Lk. 18:18-30 compared with Lk. 19:1-10). On a number of occasions we are not even told whether or not they begin to follow him or whether they recognise him as their personal saviour, or whether Jesus even asked them to. However, in whatever way people responded to Jesus, their lives were changed from that point on. Imagine if people were able to say the same about you and your group – that in you they saw a glimpse of Jesus and the kingdom of God.

The starting point of this particular book is a desire to ensure the people you meet *will* meet the God of heaven in creation – in their lives, on this earth, in the here and now. At the same time, however, it is important to recognise the significance of ensuring that the people you meet also have opportunities to meet with the God of creation in heaven, through an *eternal* life – in heaven, in the not yet.

EXPRESS EXPERIENCE

From working on the streets with young people I have found that the most helpful approach is to decide that people's response to God is not to be a condition of my involvement in their lives. That said, whatever way you finally choose to meet your community's needs, you should always include the opportunity for people to consider that a response to God is a possible solution to the condition of their lives.

INTEGRAL MISSION IN REALITY

It is time to conclude this initial section of Chapter 1, which encourages you to explore for yourself the issue of integral mission and the kingdom, before moving on to how to begin to engage with this with your group. As you do so, what you have read about the way Jesus sought to extend his kingdom through recognition, restoration and a call for response, will either leave you thinking:

- 'I knew that',
- 'I did not know that', or
- 'I realise I knew that but what I do not know is what to do about that.'

If you are left thinking the latter, then *Express Community*, and the process it suggests as a way to bring local integral mission to your life and your community's life, is just what you need.

The reality is that most of what we have explored about Jesus' life and mission in this opening burst of colour is not new, but the fact remains that most of us, if we are honest, continue to struggle to live and love in this way. Jesus' encouraging statement to his disciples in John 14:12, preparing them for his return to his heavenly kingdom, probably does not help you either: 'I tell you the truth, anyone who has faith in me will do what I have been doing. He will do even greater things than these.' Rather than encouraging you, it just leaves you with more questions, about who, what, why, where and how. Most of us do not live a kingdom life, not because we do not want to, but because we do not know how to. We are unsure who needs serving, what to do for the best, why people might want to allow us to serve them anyway or how the little we have to offer could ever be of any help. *Express Community* is a guide designed to overcome some of the barriers you may feel towards developing an integral mission within your community.

A simple way for you to begin to bless others with 'even greater things' than Jesus did is to start by focusing for now on doing some of the same things Jesus did. Allow your belief in Jesus and in his Christian community to give you the strength simply to belong with others in your wider community.

BELONG, BLESS AND BELIEVE

The ways in which Jesus chooses to extend his kingdom – recognising, restoring and responding – need to be at the heart of everything you do both as a group and as a community. As a group how can you begin to recognise needs in order to see who needs restoring and therefore how you should respond to the needs in your community? At the same time your community needs to recognise its own need, work with you to restore it, and find ways to respond appropriately to that need. Grasp this and you'll begin to grab hold of what it is that God is calling you to be. One way to interpret Jesus' integral mission for your own life in community is through seeing the need to belong with each other, to bring God's blessing to others, and to believe in and with others. That's what God's great commands are all about: loving others and loving God through action.

LEARNING FROM LIFE

A famous wildlife cameraman was once asked what the most difficult aspect of his job was. The interviewer, expecting him to say travelling, irregular hours, mosquitos or simply the dangerous situations he had had to face to get the best shot, seemed slightly shocked when he replied, 'Helplessness.'

To see a young cub lagging behind as he treks through the jungle, in danger of losing all contact with its father. To see a giraffe's newborn son struggling to get to its feet, the mother's desperate nudging of its lifeless body, knowing that if she fails, its short life will come to an end. To see a salmon loosing its spirit and strength as it consistently fails in its attempts to jump upstream to lay its eggs. These are the things that make the life of even the most professional of observers tough. The constant tension between capturing the best shot whilst all the time holding back on an overwhelming desire to drop everything to step into the frame was the hardest thing he had faced as he viewed the wonder of God's creation from behind a camera lens.

What does your image of Express Community and therefore your picture of an integral mission look like? If you were to set your life alongside Jesus', would you be able to spot the difference? Does his model of integral mission inform yours? Any change in community will only come about as you and your group allow your God to increase your contact, your compassion and your commitment. How long are you willing to continue to observe your community from a distance before you begin to take steps to see your need to belong, bless and believe?

KEY QUESTIONS

1. *Who* are you, and what do you bring to this process? What quality of relationship, recognition and contact do you have with your God, your group and your community?

2. *What* do you want to achieve as a result of the Express Community process? Do you want to see action, restoration or compassion? What about your community, your God: what do they want to see?

3. *Why* have you chosen Express Community as a process? Do you see it as a good way to approach evangelism, response and commitment within yourself, your group and your community?

4. *How* do these questions inform your vision of what you will see happen as a result of studying *Express Community*? What do your answers say about you, your group and maybe your community's potential to live with an integral mission, to reveal Jesus and to change lives?

---

[1] Photosynthesis is the process by which green plants form organic compounds from water and carbon dioxide in the presence of sunlight. See G.N. Garmonsway, *The Penguin Concise English Dictionary* (London: Bloomsbury Books, 1991).

ENGAGE YOUR GROUP
EASY-TO-USE SESSION PLANS

A MORE INTEGRAL VISION

Now that you have explored the issue of kingdom and integral mission, it is time to use what you have discovered to inform how you input these elements into your work together as a group who are seeking to express community. Each session has up to an hour-and-a-half of material, which means you are free to pick and choose what you use in response to your individual situation, both within your group and your community.

The *what* and *why* of Jesus' life, directly impact *who* he is in his community. It is important to see that these three elements are there in everything he does; they are each a part of one integral mission. The sessions that follow – belonging, blessing and believing – give just some ideas for your group as to how they may start to consider how to live a life of integral mission in the community.

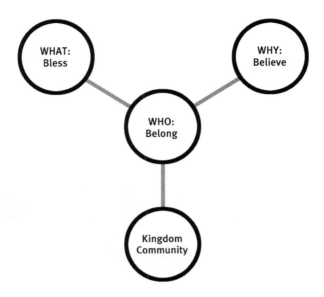

In order to recognise you need to belong

First, Jesus went to where the people were to proclaim and demonstrate the reality of God's kingly rule. Anyone who has ever tried to maintain a long-distance relationship with a girl or boyfriend, who lived overseas, studied at a different university or who lived across the other side of town will know how difficult it can be during long periods of separation. Love has first to be given before it can be received. In order to do this we must expect to be asked to take it to people, rather than expecting them to come to us. Love requires contact: it is not possible to love from a distance.

In order to restore you need to bless

Secondly, Jesus showed that the kingdom of God is about love and compassion for those in need. He demonstrated that the kingdom of God was in part about relieving suffering, recognising people's mental or physical pain and healing them. If you decide to go to where your community is, whether that's geographically, physically, mentally or down any other 'alley', it is inevitable that you will want to meet their needs. Love is a verb after all, it's active; it has to include some practical element. A card, a bunch of flowers, a shoulder to cry on, someone who will be there whatever the circumstances. Contact with your community will inevitably lead to compassion, that is human nature.

In order to respond you need to believe

Thirdly, Jesus demonstrated the kingdom in action. True love makes a real difference: when you give, it changes you; when you receive, it changes you. When people see the kingdom in all its glory, they want to turn from their past in order to discover a different future. You have to believe that who you are as a community will mean change. But first you have to be willing to change.

SESSION 1

BELONGING WITHIN COMMUNITY

Aim: To explore the concept of belonging to a community, thinking about when, where and how community happens and how this relates to the way we live our lives.

YOU WILL NEED

Bibles, photos or images of famous global or local landmarks, coloured card, *The Prince of Egypt* on video or DVD (optional)

Identikit (10 mins)

Hand out a sheet of famous landmarks and encourage your group, in pairs, to try and identify as many as they can. For example:

Worksheets are available online at www.expresscommunity.org. You could make up your own 'identikit' if you prefer to include some local landmarks.

Explain that we all recognise certain landmarks whether we've been there or not. There are probably hundreds of landmarks or distinctive features within our community, which as yet we have not really noticed. This process is designed to allow your group to begin to identify the people, places and issues at the heart of where they live.

Community is ... (20 mins)

Explain that this session will explore what it means to live in community with others. Copy the following words onto individual pieces of card and place them at the centre of the room. Gather your group around the cards.

neighbourhood, society, area, district, village, commune, public, people, population, local, zone, region, town, identity, community, friendship, sharing, helping each other, playing together, learning together, working together, eating together

Hand each person a coloured sticker or a flag (which you could make using a piece of garden cane and a sheet of gummed coloured paper) and in turn ask each person to place their 'marker' against the word or sentence which for them best describes what community is.

Encourage people to give a brief explanation of why they have chosen that particular card. You may or may not end up with a group consensus as to what they feel community is. Either way, sum up some of the points that were raised and move on to think about the types of community your group are involved in themselves.

● ●

This belongs to ... (10 mins)

As a whole group spend some time thinking about the different places or occasions when you have felt part of a community, such as a school or college, at home, at church, or at the sports club. Produce a spider diagram to illustrate your discussion:

school

church

family — community — university

swimming

football

home

orchestra

Summarise by suggesting that community exists for a number of different reasons:

● for a *purpose* – to do something together, such as sports teams, schools or colleges

● as *place* – the place you live, work or play, such as your village or town, the factory or office where you work

● because of *people* – because of shared interests, common goals or skills, taking the form of a club or a particular gang

To differing degrees different communities will exist for at least two or more of these reasons. Something like a football team, for example, involves all of these: footballers meet to play football, at a football ground, and their shared interest is sport, in this case football.

- In groups discuss other examples of communities and try to decide on the primary reasons they meet.

- See if you can prioritise their main reasons for forming by placing them into some sort of order.

- Can you think of other reasons why a community might form?

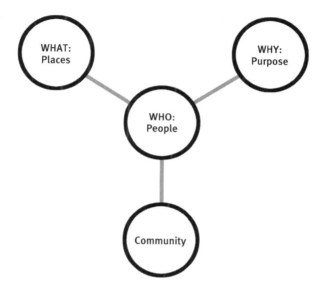

My involvement in community (10 mins)

To begin to understand how your group are involved in their different communities, hand each person a copy of the 'My involvement in the community' sheet (draw them yourselves or download from www.expresscommunity.org). These will be a useful record to keep for later when you come to think about how, when and where you can connect with your community in Chapter 3. Explain how people should fill in the sheet:

- In the central circle put your name.

- In Zone A write the activities on which you spend your time, such as in employment, child caring, watching TV, or playing sport.

- In Zone B write the people groups with which these activities bring you into contact: a parent of young children may come into contact with teachers and other parents, for instance.

- In Zone C write those issues in which you are interested or with which you are involved in some way, such as the environment, drug abuse, etc. *These are likely to be connected to Zones A and B, but occasionally people may have an interest which at present they do not spend any time on. These should be written in Zone C and a line drawn connecting it straight to the centre.*

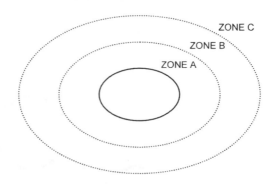

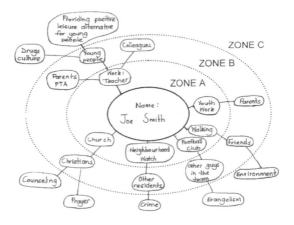

Israel united (20 mins)

In the Bible the word 'community' is used mainly with reference to the people of Israel, especially before they had a king and when they were wandering through the wilderness. Read Psalm 105, a brief summary (45 verses) of the history of Israel, or if you can get hold of it, show two contrasting clips from *The Prince Of Egypt* (Dreamworks Home Entertainment): 1) one of the scenes in which the Israelites are forced to work to build the Pharaoh's empire (either the opening scene; the scene approximately 25 minutes from the opening title; or the one which is approximately 55 minutes from the opening title); and 2) the scene in which the Israelites are finally set free to go and discover the promised land (approximately 70 minutes from the opening title).

From your discussions about why people generally form community, why do you think it was particularly important that Israel formed a community during their wilderness period?

Encourage your group to think about times when they have been forced to do something or have felt alone, or about journeys they have made and places they have felt like strangers. Just as we do, Israel formed a community:

● for a *purpose* – to do something together, for protection and for support
● because of *place* – they were the people of the desert
● because of *people* – because of their religion, their common experience of God

In groups discuss:

● What were the particular stresses and strains on their lives that caused them to form community?
● In what ways might certain stresses and strains also undermine community?
● From what you know of Israel's journey to the Promised Land, how did these stresses and strains affect their sense of community?
● How do you think the positives and negatives might relate to the communities to which you belong?

● ●

Hands together, eyes open! (10 mins)

It is important to understand that Israel was different from most communities because they understood their reason to form community primarily as a response to God's call; the desert is where the people of God are first identified as the 'called out' (*ek kalleo*, from which comes the word *ekklesia*), called out from slavery for covenant commitment to God at Sinai. As a Christian you may believe that God created the individuals who come together to form the communities to which you belong, but have you ever thought that he may have called them into being for a reason? Use the issues raised during your previous discussion to think about the things you are aware of in your community that may impact people's ability to exist together. Right at the beginning of your attempts to express community spend some time praying about ways in which you could:

● *strengthen* the people
● *serve* in the places
● *stand* for a purpose

If appropriate, spend some time feeding back some of the things you feel God may be saying. Encourage your group to form small prayer communities (groups of three would be ideal) to pray about these issues. If possible encourage them to make a commitment to their prayer community by agreeing to meet outside of your regular meetings together.

SESSION 2

BLESSING WITHIN COMMUNITY

Aim: To explore what it means to have a sense of well-being, both as individuals and as a community. To think about what the Beatitudes have to say about the need to be a blessing within our communities.

YOU WILL NEED

Bibles, individual 'well-being graphic equaliser' sheets (copy or download from www.expresscommunity.org), large poster-sized 'well-being graphic equaliser', Post-it notes

I'm H.A.P.P.Y. (5 mins)

The Bible talks an awful lot about blessing, happiness and well-being, quite often in relation to a concept called *shalom* (See Isaiah 2:2-4; 9:1-7 and 11:1-9). *Shalom* is a Hebrew word that has traditionally been translated as 'peace'. In modern-day language that word 'peace' has come to be seen as quite passive, i.e. as the absence of war or conflict. But *shalom* is a much more dynamic word than this. It is about that sense of wholeness or well-being for which many of us are searching when we are seeking happiness.

Make a list as a group of all the things that you feel contribute to your sense of well-being. In other words, what makes you happy?

HELPFUL HINT:

Your lists could include being valued, having self-esteem, security of job and home, social networks, peace, purpose, a place to call your own, health, money, food, relationships, belonging, knowing one is loved by God.

Well-being graphic equaliser (10 mins)

As you begin to consider how to express community, take some time to think about what it is that decides the way you live your life. Filling in the table overleaf may help.

Using the top eight factors from the wish list you made earlier, treat this exercise as a kind of 'well-being health check':

● Fill in the rectangular blank boxes at the top of the page with the various 'well-being factors' you thought about earlier, such as good health, friendships, success at work, etc.

Well-being factors									
+5									
+4									
+3									
+2									
+1									
0									
-1									
-2									
-3									
-4									
-5									

● Now tick the levels (from -5 to +5) for each of the factors according to where you feel you are at this present time. For instance if you are feeling very secure in your job/studies at present you may score yourself +4 for this, but -2 for self-esteem, as you're feeling quite undervalued.

● Shade in all the boxes you have ticked to give you a clear picture of what motivates you and how you are feeling.

Think of this as your *well-being graphic equaliser* (a graphic equaliser is a device on a stereo for lowering or boosting particular frequencies). If you were able to sum up how you were currently feeling into a sound, this is how it might look on paper.

HELPFUL HINT:

It may be appropriate to share your feelings as a group; however nobody should feel pressured to do so. Getting hold of a number of different instruments and asking individuals to choose one which best expresses how they're sounding might help to bring this simple activity alive and avoid people feeling awkward about speaking around delicate issues.

Common people (5 mins)

Many people within your community will have many of the same feelings and the same motives as you do, and they may even share similar frustrations. We ought not to see these as problems but as potential opportunities to serve each other. That's why the word 'involvement' is key; it's not about you serving them in order that they may discover their sense of well-being, but about each of us serving each other. Some of the most effective community involvement will be the type that's about mutual growth, learning together and sometimes even failing together. The challenge for any effective life within community will be to begin to understand how to make connections between what people feel and what the Bible says about those feelings.

Blessed be your name? (30 mins)

Read Matthew 5:1-11 together. Divide your group into eight separate groups and hand each new group a pile of Post-it notes and an envelope containing one of the following key words taken from the passage:

poor (v. 3), mourn (v. 4), meek (v. 5), righteousness (v. 6), merciful (v. 7), heart (v. 8), peacemakers (v. 9), and persecuted (v. 10)

In just one minute write as many different words as you can that you associate with your key word. Write each word on a separate Post-it note.

After a minute bring the group back together. *Beforehand, prepare a large well-being graphic equaliser to display on the wall or floor. Each square of the grid should be the exact size of a Post-it note.* Write each of the eight key words from the passage into the 'well-being factors' box across the top. For each key word read out all the associated Post-its and as a group debate whether they are positive or negative. Positive ones should be stuck in the top half of the grid and negative ones in the bottom. At the end work out the difference between positive and negative Post-its and see how you score for each factor.

Read Matthew 5:1-11 again and this time, using the following questions to help you, discuss each verse in turn:

● What words did you associate with the verse?

● What do you feel Jesus was talking about when he said ....
(insert the key word or phrase from each verse).

● How do think being .... (insert the key word or phrase) would lead to you feeling blessed or happy, and therefore contribute to your sense of well-being?

DISCUSSION POINTERS:

Poor in spirit (v. 3): In Old Testament times the materially poor came to be identified with those who were dependent on God. With nowhere else to turn, they recognised their need of God, whereas the rich and powerful preferred to trust in their wealth and power. People expected the kingdom of heaven to be attained by merit (the Pharisees) or by fighting (the zealots). How does what Jesus says about who can enter the kingdom of heaven compare with the messages Christians give today?

Those who mourn (v. 4): Luke 19:41-42; Psalm 119:136; Ezekiel 9:4; and Philippians 3:18 might help. Are there areas of your life or community which you are, or should be, saddened by? *Images or cuttings from the local news may help to stimulate your group's thinking.*

Meek (v. 5): Meekness is often seen as weakness: however the Greek adjective *pruas* means, 'gentle', 'humble', 'considerate', or 'courteous'. Descriptions of Moses (Num. 12:3) and Jesus (Mt. 11:29) both use the same word used in the Beatitudes.

Hunger and thirst for righteousness (v. 6): There is no distinction in Hebrew and Greek between 'righteousness' and 'justice'. They are both about hungering for a right relationship with God and striving for what is right and just for others.

Pure in heart (v. 8): The heart in the Bible is not the seat of emotions but the centre of who we are as human beings. It controls the way we think, the way we act and the way we feel.

Peacemakers (v. 9): 1 Peter 3:11; Hebrews 12:14; and Romans 12:18 might help. Consider the difference between 'peace-keeping' and 'peace-making'.

Persecuted (v. 10): In what ways might living out the Beatitudes bring you more/less persecution? Why, and how willing are you to accept this prospect?

• •

Dark and light (10 mins)

- In what ways are the well-being factors Jesus talks about in the Beatitudes different from/similar to the list you made earlier?

- What is important about the fact that Jesus' well-being factors are all about giving, whereas when most people think about happiness they think about getting or owning? Are we striving for what Jesus says we should be striving for?

- What do you think Jesus meant when he said, 'You are the light of the world' (v. 14)?

Although thinking of our community as dark is not always helpful, by suggesting that we are 'the light of the world' (v. 14) Jesus might be suggesting that our communities are a little 'dull' and in need of something to make them brighter. The question is what? Do these new concepts of happiness offer new ideas about how we should be expressing community?

Return to your individual and the large well-being graphic equaliser and consider what impact: 1) your original well-being factors might have on your community – are the results positive or negative? and 2) the Beatitude well-being factors might have on your community – are the results positive or negative?

• •

Needs must (5 mins)

Need is more than just material poverty. Someone may have a very strong sense of well-being and yet be living in poor housing, and another person may have all their material needs met, and yet have a very low sense of well-being. Outward appearances of material wealth can also be misleading. Often poor housing estates have a higher proportion of satellite dishes than the wealthier suburbs, but this is reflective of the desperate need for cheap entertainment to absorb the large amounts of unwanted leisure time and the inaccessibility of more affluent leisure pursuits (such as holidays, cinema, etc). People's sense of well-being is, however, affected by their environment, and one factor (e.g. unemployment) may negatively affect many other aspects of their life (such as self-esteem, relationships, and an overall sense of purpose).

Your group needs to be actively working towards promoting all the aspects of *shalom,* both within the group itself as well as within the community. Meaningful and valued relationships with others must be based on *shalom* rather than some narrower agenda of meeting solely spiritual or physical need; only then will people begin to experience what it means to receive God's true blessing.

SESSION 3

BELIEVING WITHIN COMMUNITY

Aim: To develop a clear understanding of how Christians are called to live within community and to understand the purpose this has.

YOU WILL NEED

Bibles, one old shoebox for each member of your group (local shops should have some, or ask people to bring their own if it's easier. The older and more damaged the better; make sure you recycle them afterwards!), a selection of popular magazines and/or newspapers, glue, pens, marker pens, enough stones for each group member (optional)

• •

Living stones – people (5 mins)

As you begin, pass around a container full of stones and ask each individual to pick out a stone which they feel relates somehow to them. *Things people might look for are stones with certain textures, marks or patterns, different shapes or features that express how they may be feeling, thinking or see themselves.*

Explain that in 1 Peter 2, Peter refers to Christians as living stones. At this point you may want to split the group into threes. Or remain as a whole if you feel that it would be more appropriate. Read out 1 Peter 2:1-12 and then ask the group to consider why Jesus might describe his followers in this way; do that by using the following discussion points. The aim of this part of the session is to consider in what ways the image of individual living stones (v. 4) relates to the idea that the purpose of the Christian community is in part about how we relate to God.

DISCUSSION POINTERS:

● List all the different qualities of stones.

● What are the characteristics of something that is living? In what way do you think verses 1-3 are significant?

● Add these things together; why do you think Peter connects these two in this way?

BIBLICAL BACKGROUND

Rather than stones, Jesus uses the analogy of a rock in Matthew 7:24-27 in the story of the wise and foolish builders. Why? In what ways do you think this relates to the significance of which foundation each individual living stone chooses to build his or her life upon? What are the potential consequences of these choices – both positive and negative?

Spritual house – place (20 mins)

Dump a huge pile of shoeboxes in the centre of your space. Divide your group into twos and ask each pair to choose a shoebox. Hand out a selection of popular magazines and/or newspapers, glue and pens. Encourage them to produce a collage on one side of their shoebox based on how they see their role in the Christian community, within this group, within their CU, or at their church. After 15 minutes ask people to finish off. Encourage each person to feedback what they have produced and why. Take the shoeboxes and stack them together to start to build the individual 'stones' into a wall. Soon you'll begin to see a picture building of what happens to Christian community when individual living stones come together.

Read out 1 Peter 2:1-12 again, asking your group to listen carefully as you do so. Here Peter starts to build a picture of what a Christian community may be all about.

The aim of this part of the session is to consider in what ways the images of individual living stones (v. 4) joining to form a spiritual house (v. 5) relates to the idea that the Christian community may be about how we relate to each other, as well as how we relate to God.

DISCUSSION POINTERS:

● What are the strengths that stones provide when they come together?*(For example, they get stronger, offer security, are more supportive, provide protection, etc.)*

● Using examples from your wall of shoeboxes, in what ways are the individual living stones different?

● In what ways do they complement each other when they join together?

● What are the potential weaknesses of joining together? In what ways can you work together as a group to try and eliminate these?

As Christians we are all part of the one 'building' when we join together. A stone standing by itself is pretty useless. We cannot be Christians in isolation – we must be together in community. Though when we think of walls we're used to seeing structures built from near perfect bricks or stones, in Old Testament times and even today in more traditional dry stone walls we can see how individual stones of all different sizes and shapes come together to form something of worth. Each had a role; each has a place. Despite what others think of us, there is a unique place in God's plan for all of us, which begins to take shape when we are with others.

BIBLICAL BACKGROUND

People rejected Jesus and yet he turned out to be the most important stone of all. Peter describes Jesus as the cornerstone who keeps the temple together. A cornerstone is a large stone supporting two walls at right angles to each other.

The temple was the holiest and most important place for all Jews; it was seen as the dwelling place of God. People from all over the known world would travel to the temple to worship God.

A temple or spiritual house in and of itself is not especially important. It exists so that people can meet with God. The Christian community of believers exists so that others can come and worship God as well.

• •

Royal priesthood – purpose (15 mins)

So far Peter's pictures of a Christian community have included individual living stones joining together to form a spiritual house (v. 5), but for what purpose? The aim of this part of the session is to think about how Peter's image of a holy/royal priesthood (v. 9) may help to understand that Christian community is about:

- how we relate to those outside of the Christian community
- how we relate to each other
- how we relate to God

BIBLICAL BACKGROUND

The task of the order of priests whom Peter knew best was to be go-betweens between God and the people of Israel. They kept the temple going in Jerusalem. They took the sacrifices of the people and presented them on the altar to God on their behalf. They took the people's tithes and gave them to the poor.

DISCUSSION POINTERS:

- Thinking back to your individual shoeboxes, which are now an integral part of a wall, what do you understand the role of the Christian community to be when it joins together?

- In what ways may there be parallels between the holy priesthood and your group or community of believers?

- The purpose of the priesthood is 'to offer spiritual sacrifices acceptable to God through Jesus Christ' (Rom. 12:1; Phil. 4:14-18; Heb. 13:15-16). What do you think the spiritual sacrifices you have to offer might be?

- What insights does this give you in to the role of your group of Christian believers?

HELPFUL HINT:

Note how the spiritual sacrifice of living a life that glorifies God and blesses our neighbour parallels the Old Testament priesthood role of presenting sacrifices to God and giving tithes to the poor.

BIBLICAL BACKGROUND

By the time Peter was writing, the worship of the Roman Emperors as gods had developed so that in every corner of the empire there would be a shrine and a priesthood that was devoted specifically to their worship. These priests, as representatives of the dictator who ruled over the empire, were royal priests.

With these priests in mind, maybe, Peter says that every Christian is a royal priest – a priest that represents the King of Kings in the world, whose function is to declare Jesus as the one who has all authority in heaven and earth. As Christians, we are to show by the quality of our lives, our prayer, our worship and service that the earth and its people really belong to God. The community in which we live really belongs to God, so if we ignore it we are ignoring God's rightful possession.

A holy nation (10 mins)

Peter provides an ever-expanding vision of 'believing within a Christian community'. It starts with individuals (living stones), who together are able to form their own community (a house), the purpose of which is to serve others (holy/royal priests). At every stage of this Express Community process, the key to your progress will be how prepared you are to focus on:

● building relationships with God;
● building relationships with members of your group/Christian community/church;
● building relationships with your community.

Peter's final picture of Christian community is a holy nation (v. 9): what do you think he means by this?

BIBLICAL BACKGROUND

Such language as a 'holy nation' would immediately remind the Jews of their own history. In the Old Testament what made the nation of Israel distinctive was the fact that they had been saved out of slavery in Egypt. However, God did not just call Israel for his own sake or for their sake but for the sake of all nations. They were to be light for the Gentiles.

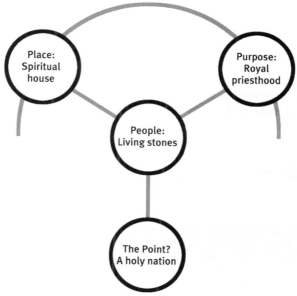

DISCUSSION POINTERS:

● Given this background, in what ways is the Christian community called to be different from the world?

● What is the purpose of the Christian community being different? What might these differences mean to your community?

● In what ways might you 'declare the praises of him who called you' (v. 9) in your community?

● ●

Facing a brick wall (15-25 mins)

WHAT ARE YOU BUILDING?

All the pictures Peter uses in 1 Peter 2:1-12 demonstrate that the Christian community exists for the sake of others. Conclude the session by asking your group to:

1) Summarise the role of the Christian community.

2) Discuss how Peter's pictures fit with their own experience of the Christian community.

This session has focused primarily on the positive aspects of stones joining together, i.e. that together they provide strength and support, but what about weaknesses? Rather than providing strength, some of these elements that describe a Christian community act as barriers to God's blessing. On the reverse of each of the individual shoeboxes write down some of the things that might prevent others from joining the Christian community.

3) In what ways can the Christian community being different from the world sometimes lead to isolation from the world? What are the positives and negatives of being different?

4) Do the sins of verse 1 get in the way of our ability to express community? If so, how do they, and what can be done about it?

WHAT NEEDS BREAKING?

As your group stare at the reverse of the wall, it will give them a powerful image of what people outside the Christian community often see. Their view of Christians, and the good stuff on the inside, is often obscured because of what they see on the outside. This affects how they think of God. As the group reflect on this, ask them to spend some time considering some of the things they could do to help break down some of the barriers that may exist between their Christian community and their wider community. As you stand together, read verses from the Bible over each individual and the wall (for example, Eph. 4:1-3; Gal. 5:16-26; 1 Cor. 13:1-13; or Jn. 15:1-17, especially v. 13).

Allow a time of extended silence. Pray that God would speak clearly to you and your group about things you need either to do or stop doing in order to begin to break down the barriers. After a suitable period of time hand out as much scrap paper as you can get your hands on and, using marker pens, write down God's response to your prayers – use a separate sheet for each point. Encourage the group to feedback what God has been saying. Make a record of it for use later in the Express Community process. You may like to use the 'stepping stones' below to sort your thoughts into things to think about, things to find out, and things to do.

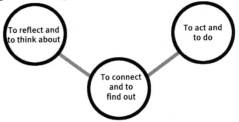

Screw up the paper and symbolically throw it at the wall to try to knock it down. This session may have seemed heavy for some, so finish on a high note with some fun!

THE NEED TO REBUILD?

You may find that this is an appropriate place to end or you may finish by rebuilding your walls. This time make different structures, which represent how your group feel they should connect with their community and their community with them. Let your group decide, or make some suggestions – a bridge is an obvious one. You could emphasise the need to have Jesus at the centre as the capstone who holds the whole structure in place. Turn it into a challenge; make it fun!

Jesus

EXPRESS TOGETHER

What insights have you gained about the kingdom of God through these sessions? How do you and your group need to change in order to reflect more of God's kingdom?

BELONGING WITHIN COMMUNITY

At this stage it is important that you record and begin to communicate your thoughts regarding *Express Community*. Encourage your group, and of course yourself, to begin to keep a personal journal. 'What happened today', overleaf, is designed to help your group to record some of their thoughts during the day or week. Hopefully it will provide a useful resource for them to remember the people who inspired them, the people who made them cry, the things said during a session, or their observations made within their community. Encourage people to take another step with their thinking. In the, 'So I think that . . .' section invite them to think about what God might be saying to them as a result of their experience.

Most people will find that writing any kind of diary requires self-discipline. Here are a few handy hints to help you and your group get going:

- Push yourself at the start to see if you can get into doing it.
- Draw on the encouragement of other members of your group.
- Get everyone to write together.
- Do not do it because you think you have to.
- Do not try too hard if you are feeling tired.

Naturally, encouraging your group members to share anything from their journal at the beginning of each session will encourage them to keep a journal. Hearing of one another's progress will also provide encouragement to the whole group.

What happened today

The detail (what, when, where, why and who):

Which left me feeling ...

So I think that ...

BLESSING WITHIN COMMUNITY

Even though you've just begun, it is not too early to start recording your thoughts about blessing your community. Why not encourage each person in your group to consider the Lord's Prayer and write the prayer from the perspective of different individuals or groups from within the community of which they are aware? What would it mean for the kingdom of God to come for:

- the homeless person?
- the single parent?
- the harassed shopkeeper?
- the teenage girl who hangs about on street corners?
- the lads who race their motorbikes across the fields every night?
- the elderly lady who's afraid to come out of her house?

At some point it may be appropriate to share the prayers as a whole group, or even with the wider church.

BELIEVING WITHIN COMMUNITY

Whatever you feel God is calling your group to do as part of *Express Community*, if you are part of a wider Christian community, such as a church, cell-group network, or Christian Union, then you will need to consider how what you are doing fits in to their overall vision for community. Now may be an appropriate time to consider inviting the leadership along to one of your sessions to discuss your feelings and initial thoughts about integral mission and Express Community. Are there ways in which they can stay informed, become inspired or get involved?

A good start would be to buy for the leadership, or get them to buy, a copy of this book. That way they will know exactly the process you are going through. Regular updates with you as the leader and with your group will also be key. Perhaps as you finish each stage you could arrange for them to join you for an informal chat or ask whether at suitable points in the process you could present your thoughts to the leadership or the wider Christian community that they represent. It may be that the wider Christian community to which you belong would like to go through the process with you: *Express Community* has already been used effectively in church-based home/cell groups with adults aged 20 to 50.

Alternatively, Tearfund's *Church Community and Change* is available as a resource for churches considering community development amongst the poorest of the poor in their community. For more information, email ccc@tearfund.org, call 0845 355 8355 (ROI 00 44 845 355 8355).

He has showed you, O man, what is good. And what does the LORD require of you? To **act justly** and to **love mercy** and to **walk humbly** with your God (Mic. 6:8).

Chapter 2

SO WHAT DOES THE LORD REQUIRE?

Gymnastics, skating and even musical statues: they all require some sense of balance to master them. Somehow, just when you think you've cracked it, you lose all sense of co-ordination and perspective of what was needed and the whole thing comes tumbling down. For some people, balance is natural; others have to work at it. As Christians we are told not to worry about a thing – what we eat, what we drink or what to wear (Mt. 6:25), and yet we get things all mixed up too. We should be the most balanced people on the planet. Are you? Are your group? Jesus came to put everything in our lives into perspective, turning the world on its head, or rather putting it back on its feet. He changed the way the world judged success. Jesus says in Luke 12:15 that 'a man's [or for that matter, a woman's] life does not consist in the abundance of his possessions', and yet few of us live as though we believe it!

The majority of us live our lives at a hundred miles an hour, every day is like a land speed record attempt, getting there as quick as we can, however we can, in the ridiculous hope that we'll somehow beat yesterday's Personal Best. You might argue that this does not describe the people in your group. They're so balanced they're horizontal. They would grab any chance they could to lay back rather than run around a track, to stay in bed rather than race ahead, or even go nowhere rather than be somewhere. A quick check-up may indeed suggest this to be the case. However, a more careful, thorough medical may reveal that though many of them might like to sit and stand slowly, they still expect the world to move around them at some degree of knots.

If your group are lethargic, use this to your advantage. In order to get the best out of this stage of *Express Community*, i.e. in order to really engage in Reflecting within Community, you're going to have to slow down completely, ease off the gas, put your foot on the brake, take a step back and remove your hands from some of the things that you have (or want to have) that you feel are precious and meaningful to your life. That way your hands will be freer to invest in something significant and special for the sake of others. Following Jesus is not easy; often he relies on you being prepared to give up more in order to take on less. *Express Community* is about being prepared to lay aside any previous assumptions about your life and the life of your community in order to develop a more integral view of mission, potentially including the kind of service and sacrifice that Jesus' life involved. As its title suggests, this chapter is particularly significant in the process of reflection because it opens with the questions most of us dare not ask for fear of the answers. 'God, who are you, what do you want me to do with my life, why and how?'

WHAT IS YOUR EXPERIENCE OF A BALANCED LIFE?

Being prepared to check in with the Bible regularly in order to get checked out by God is going to be hard. It will take time and you may feel you are delaying the Express Community process by doing so. Rest assured: you are not. Checking whether you need to change is completely necessary if you are successfully to make your most effective community connection. It is doubtful that anyone in your group will relish the thought of standing before God waiting for their baggage to arrive in full view of you and the rest of your group. Seeing the sticky tape patching the outside, hoping the multicoloured 'Jesus loves me' strap is secure enough to keep all your dirty laundry on the inside. The truth is that because Jesus loves you, he wants to release you from the unhelpful stuff you have packed into your life so far – the stuff that weighs you down, preventing you reaching your full potential. Opening up to him and others may be the only way to lighten the load. Max Lucado explains in his book *Just Like Jesus*: 'God loves you just the way you are, but he refuses to leave you that way. He wants you to be just like Jesus.'[1]

You may find it hard going, particularly as group leader, when people begin to realise how far off the mark they are. Even in the knowledge of what God says he requires for better community living, some people will refuse to change. They are happy with their life just the way it is. They want it, it's theirs and they don't care who gets in the way as they push aside people in order to get it. Others may find they have totally misunderstood God's calling but do not know where to go; they are worried that because they got it wrong, that's it and there's no going back.

Well, the intention of this chapter is not to tear strips off people and ridicule the things that have become important to them, or close to their hearts, but to help them to reconsider what their heart's desire might be in the light of what the Bible says about reflecting Jesus within community. Thankfully the Bible's positive critique, unlike some of the negative criticism your group will have received over the years, has great advice on how to fix things. Encourage people not to get too disheartened and try to enable them to be honest and open to change. At the same time recognise that some people need space to reflect by themselves.

Ever feel like life is just one endless game of cramming, craving and crashing? As well as picking up baggage during our travels we treat other areas of our life like a challenge rather than a calling. We cram and crave as much as we can, regardless of who is in front of us in the queue and the effect it has on them. Of course this metaphor depends on your culinary tastes, but at some point in your life you've probably had a stuffed crust at your local pizzeria. No? Well then, perhaps you prefer a Margherita, ham and mushroom? Or spicy chicken? Maybe you simply can't decide and so always plump for one of those 'eat-as-much-as-you-like' deals: you know the sort, where you get the chance to break the record for filling the world's smallest bowl with as much food as you can, whilst at the same time jostling for position with the local rugby team out on their bimonthly binge. The sudden rush for the line as the waiter brings out the fresh pizzas, pasta and Parmesan. It may be 'all you can eat' but to look at some people's bowls as they leave the buffet cart you'd think it was 'all you can eat per visit'! Cramming in what we can, when we can, regardless of the effect it has on others – or even ourselves – is how most of us live our lives. Stuff the consequences, we want what we feel is rightfully ours, plus whatever extra toppings we can grab along the way.

Not content with sheer quantity, having the 'next best thing' is also many people's personal goal for life. Whatever you managed to forget as you left the school gates on your last day – algebra, bacteria, or Caligula – no doubt you will be able to recall with some accuracy the seasonal crazes that rushed through the yard like a bad case of British Bulldog. In many ways school is the practice ground for life's constant collection fads: though we may have grown out of football stickers, yo-yos or Cyber Pets, who can resist that latest mobile phone which lets you scan, fax, photocopy and email all for the price of a small-sized family car? We find value in having the latest gadget, thing or accessory; it makes us feel worth more, regardless of how worthless it may have made the person who picked, produced or packed it. As you begin to express community you will be faced with some tough choices about your life in relation to others. Do you sacrifice your own cravings for the sake of the needs of others, or do you simply steam ahead before it's too late? Perhaps it is time we said 'enough is enough'. As leaders, maybe God is calling us to be trendsetters rather than trendchasers.

So why do so many of us try and cram in as many possessions or experiences as we can? The truth is that despite what Jesus says in Luke 12:15, that 'a man's life does not consist in the abundance of his possessions', at the end of the day that is how many of us judge our success. We talk about the value of simply being, but if we are honest most of us still find worth in what we do, are and have. Why else is the question, 'So what do you do for a living?' one of the first of three question we ask people when we meet them? The others being 'why' they're here and 'what' their name is. Often as leaders we are the best at being busy, asking what, why and how, before we have even considered that what we should really be asking, and what God wants to know, is 'Who am I?' and 'Who are you?' Do not get too downhearted; success itself is not necessarily a problem. God only disapproves of us when we do not use the resources he has given us wisely. It pains him when he sees people getting more and more at the expense of others. The danger of filling your life with as many things as possible, hoping it will add to a sense of well-being, is that it often only serves to make us so self-absorbed that we:

- forget to consider how our decisions may affect others
- feel worthless because we have so much and still do not feel good, and
- feel worthless, believing that compared to others we've got nothing

The danger is that living this way means you'll eventually crash. Every person is built with a certain capacity to give, get and go, and once it becomes too much it is difficult to see anything clearly. Your view on the reason for life's journey becomes obscured, like a driver hampered by fog. Lose the focus of your life for a minute and you might find yourself hitting a brick wall, or worse still, someone else! Your immediate response may be to begin to think of endless excuses for why things are going or have gone wrong, blaming others for your blunders, botches and bad choices. But the fact is that, however many times we try to use those 'in an attempt to kill a fly, I drove into a telephone pole' type of insurance claim excuses, most crashes are down to driver error. Admit it, you were not concentrating; you were not focused on God's heart for his people. But before we get on to God's heart, let's focus for a moment on his people.

WHAT IS MOST PEOPLE'S EXPERIENCE
OF A BALANCED LIFE?

A quick glance at the evening news, newspaper or email and you will soon realise that the world is full of injustice and imbalance. But how connected to the issues do we really feel, or do the images begin to disappear from our mind even before we've switched channel, turned the page or closed the file? Are our young people grieved by the fact that according to the Department for International Development (DFID) one in five children of primary school age living in the developing world do not attend school?[2] Does the fact that 1.1 billion people in the world struggle to survive on less than 70p per day influence how people in this country live their lives?[3] We live in what many call a global community, in which the choices we make on the high street impact people as far away as Afghanistan, Burkina Faso or Cuba.

As people become more aware of the ethical issues surrounding things such as food, fashion and finance, and the connection they have with the person who has grown, sewn or loaned their possessions, how much more should they feel a link between themselves and the people they work, study and live with in their community. Just look at the rise in Fairtrade goods stocking our shelves these days.[4]

As we live in a global community, the lifestyle choices we make do impact people with whom we share this world. If people are beginning to recognise this on a global scale, what are the consequences nationally and locally? *Express Community is primarily concerned with connecting with the inequalities that exist in our own communities.* Thirteen million children in the UK (one in three) are unable to enjoy a standard of living that is considered minimal by our government: they are denied the comforts, benefits and inclusion that many of us take for granted. One in 20 of all people in the UK are likely to experience homelessness at some time in their lives.[5] You may come and go through the doorway of your favourite fast-food restaurant by day without realising that by night there's every chance it may become the resting place of the heads of some young homeless couple. Occasionally you hear of shootings on the street, teenagers being stabbed to death at school or children taken from outside the 'safety' of their own homes. You may say these are rare occurrences, but try telling that to the loved ones they leave behind. What about the elderly, single parents, the mentally unwell? What do you know about the really marginalised people around us everywhere? Poverty in your community may be different from that which exists overseas, but the result is the same: isolation, desperation, pain, hurt and powerlessness. Like it or not, as you engage with people in your community, you are going to have to face up to some of these issues, asking questions about where it all went wrong, redressing the balance in their favour and sometimes holding your hands up and admitting you were partly to blame.

Some of the blame for injustice at the heart of our communities lies firmly at our feet. If not us personally, then people like us. People who, spending so much of their lives packing things in, are by and large busy ignoring or at least missing out people with less – people with problems, pains or personal issues that all need resolving. Some people come out with statements like: 'It's all their own fault;' 'They should get a job;' or 'They should not have left home in the first place.' Apart from being if not just plain ignorant, then certainly simplistic, and conveniently sidestepping any notion of our responsibilities towards one another as members of society, such expressions also condemn people to remain in the situations in which we find them: nothing can change when we do not believe in people. It does not matter whose fault it may or not be; the question is: what are you going to do about it? If our motivation comes out of a love for God and a love for others, then our minds should be different, transformed by Christ (Rom. 12:2). Even if others do argue that the poor and persecuted are largely responsible for their own mess, love offers solutions through compassion not condemnation.

One of our major problems in life is that when we come to weigh up what lifestyle choices we should make, the last thing on our minds is others. The first thing is ourselves. In this technologically abundant world, people are less concerned about what their actions may take from the lives of others, but more with what it adds to theirs. Your average set of digitally enhanced scales may be accurate to the nearest nanogram but they provide no counter-weight to measure anything against. At the risk of sounding old, they do not make scales like they used to, where the process of measuring itself was concerned with maintaining balance, by seeking equality on both sides, maintaining fairness for those that have and those that do not, and restoring justice for all. It is no coincidence that a set of scales is the internationally recognised symbol of justice. Justice is about equality. Could these scales be what God had in mind when he talked about living a life that restored justice – scales that measure how we live in the context of who he has called us to be?

WHAT IS GOD'S IDEA OF A BALANCED LIFE?

The Express Community process is designed to refocus your thinking, opening your eyes on a world that is stacked against some and weighted in favour of others. A life of integral mission will find ways to connect with people in order to set about restoring fairness to their sometimes fragile lives. The Bible offers a different way of weighing up your life, a different way to restore the balance and recapture your focus. Micah 6:8 asks the question what is it that God wants, and then replies with three simple phrases which together form one integral call to live life differently: to 'act justly', to 'love mercy' and to 'walk humbly with your God'.

Rather than measuring success by our own achievements, it may be time to return to those more traditional methods – weighing our actions against a counter-weight that asks how just, merciful and humble we are. As we weigh up our lives we should seek to hold in balance the effect it has on others and what the Bible says about that. Anyone who has tried to read the Bible in a year knows just how substantial it is as a way to counterbalance the culture many of us find ourselves living in. God's way of measuring our lives is concerned with measuring what we have or do not have, do or do not do, against the effect it has on others. It is our Christian responsibility to see that justice is done within our community. Surely this is the way to restore people to their ultimate glory, by returning to a more balanced life that uses God's requirement for our lives to further our knowledge about how to return to his will.

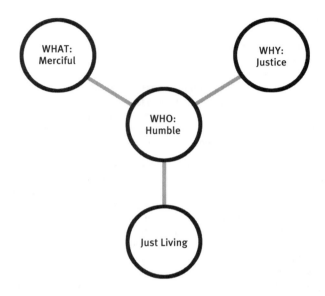

JUSTICE

Believe it or not some people find Christianity off-putting. For some it is the endless meetings, for others it is because they feel there are too many rules. How else do you account for responses such as, 'I could never live up to that;' 'I could not possibly do that;' or 'I could not possibly *not* do that.' In reality there are not that many laws and most are just a matter of common sense. The Bible does talk about a number of different types of laws: the top 10 are probably the most famous (Ex. 20:1-17), where again we see an emphasis on loving God and loving others. The following types are particularly significant if we are to live with a more community-focused view of life:

1. 'Wet paint rules': those that are for your own good; keep them or you risk harming yourself (e.g. Ex 23:12; Deut. 5:12; 23:21-3; 24:5, 8);

2. 'Keep off the grass rules': those are for the good of something or someone else; keep them or risk damaging it/them (e.g. Ex. 21:12-25; 23:1-9; Deut. 20:19; 21:1-4; 22:1-4; 23:12-14; 24:12; 25:13-16).

Both are about loving God and loving others. The law God revealed to Moses on the mountain top was never meant to be about 'God the killjoy', some kind of heavenly parent playing his 'I'm older, therefore respect me' card. It was and still is good advice to a group of people just beginning to express community together. Most of the law is about God's demand for justice. His primary concern is to make sure things equal out, to make sure that our lives are not imbalanced, so the lives of others are balanced. His advice in Exodus 22:21; 23:9 and 12 and Leviticus 19:33-34 on how to include and not exclude people from their community, is just one of many lessons Israel would have learnt from its time as foreigners in Egypt. What experiences of your life affect the way you treat others? Are we always willing to learn from bad experiences or does history sometimes have a habit of repeating itself? What can we do to prevent this happening in our lives within community? God wanted to ensure Israel would neither experience nor exercise injustice in the future as they had encountered it in the past – a new sort of 'Living within community' built on fairness rather than fear. From hygiene to health, honour to happiness, it's all about a law for life.

The great commandment described by Jesus in Matthew 22:35-39 is of course his summary of what the Old Testament law was all about. It highlights that God's concern is for his people to love him and love others, and that this is the way to restore justice in our communities. In essence it is about restoring balance, returning to how things should be and treating others as you would want to be treated. Ultimately the cross was the supreme manifestation of God's justice, whilst at the same time a demonstration of his love and mercy. Perhaps if people think there are too many rules in Christianity it's because we've given them that impression. As we begin to express community it might be time to hold our hands up and say we are sorry if we have given the wrong impression about Christianity. If we have focused too much on how to behave, let's begin to find more ways to belong, bless and believe in a way that's beneficial to all.

MERCY

Jesus came to fulfil the law God gave to Israel at Sinai (Mt. 5:17). He came to show people what it meant to build a truly 'just' life; he used the strong foundations of God's law of justice as the place to start. In reality, however, his message was largely misunderstood. As we have seen already in Session 3, in 1 Peter 2:7 we are told that although he is the key to life, he was rejected. Unlike many of his contemporaries, Jesus' brand of justice offered compassion rather than condemnation as the way to restore life's balance. Session 5 explores John 8:1-11 as just one occasion when Jesus chooses to show more mercy to someone who had done wrong, despite demands from others to show less. To have any impact on people's lives in our communities we have to do more than disturb the surface by throwing about accusations. Reconciliation only emerges through the grace and mercy found in the depths of forgiveness. Jesus never says it is right to do wrong but neither does he correct without compassion. His method of guidance is one of grace and mercy rather than guilt and blame. As we seek to express what it means to be living within community, whatever 'wrongs' we do discover need to be understood in the context of people's lives – handled sensitively and then shown the same kind of mercy as Jesus showed. Stage Two: Connecting within Community will be key to informing your understanding of your community.

HUMILITY

So how do we respond to injustice in our community – with anger? Whilst there is such a thing as righteous anger, one that leads to action on behalf of those unjustly treated there is a danger that anger simply creates more suffering. Star Wars fan or not, whatever you think about it, Yoda's words in Episode I, *The Phantom Menace*, are profound: 'Anger leads to hate, hate leads to suffering' – an incredible piece of advice from one so small![6] Think of Moses' reaction to injustice in Exodus 2:11-15 and the consequences of his murder of an Egyptian for beating a fellow Hebrew. Uncontrollable anger is not God's way to restore his balance to life. Whenever we are faced with any sense of injustice within our communities, getting angry is not the answer: anger can lead to hate and hate often leads to even more suffering.

There are no quick fixes. Whatever injustice we see in our community, the delusion that we have been given some sort of divine authority to charge in and fix it is simply not acceptable. God's guidance is crucial when we are faced with examples of injustice. Pointing out faults may well be part of what God calls you to do in your community, but it must always be done in humility. Be aware that any transgressions you do spot may well be the result of how you are choosing to live your life rather than simply how someone else is choosing to live theirs. As a leader you'll probably know that when God speaks into a situation it can often be the person he speaks to that needs to take action. Always remember not to 'think of yourself more highly than you ought' (Rom. 12:3). It is sometimes easier to raise a finger to point out the need for justice in the lives of others than it is to recognise areas of injustice that may be pointing back at us. What parent has not reminded their child of this when he has slipped back into the habit of pointing the finger at others instead of admitting the fault as his own? Being a Christian does not mean we are any better than others; it just means we have accepted God's willingness to suffer the consequences of our past and admitted we need his help for the future.

KEY QUESTIONS

1. *Who* do you think God sees when he weighs you up? In what ways does he/does he not see someone after his own heart? On a scale of 0-10, how just, merciful and humble are you, your group, or your church community? In what ways are you different depending on who you are with? Why?

2. *What* do you understand by the word 'just'? In what ways have you considered it may refer to simplicity as well as fairness? In what ways do you feel the two may be integral? How might this inform how you judge, treat and feel about people?

3. *Why* do you think of your community in the way you do? What do you think of them? In what ways are your assumptions about others influenced by a lack of knowledge about their situation? What could you do to begin to increase your awareness? Why do you imagine this is important in building the foundations of a 'just' life, if at the end of this Express Community process you are going to try and build a better way of simply living within community?

4. Finally, *how* will living this way change you, your group or your community? How have you been challenged; what might change; what might continue? How will you ensure that this happens? What structure may you need to put in place? How accountable do you and your group feel towards each other? What could you do to 'just' check your actions?

ENGAGE YOUR GROUP
EASY-TO-USE SESSION PLANS

RETURNING TO A BALANCED LIFE

Living justly is the best way, the only way, to demonstrate and fulfil your and God's purpose for *Living within Community*. True justice should impact your life as much as it should others'. The following session plans are designed to engage your group in a process that will enable them to begin to redress the balance of their lives. This will not be easy, since living a life based on justice, mercy and humility are not natural but supernatural concepts. God's word and spirit are therefore crucial elements to build into the Express Community process. Change needs to happen inwardly – that is, in you and your group – before it can ever happen outwardly in community. Fixing your eyes on Jesus at every stage of this process is the only way this is possible. Galatians 5:22 offers one of God's many biblical guidelines for 'just' living. Our ability, and the ability of our community, to refocus will depend on the values by which we live. A kingdom community will explore together how to use the freedom that it has to manage the balance between doing whatever it wants and doing what is best for God and others. It will aim to:

- speak of love and compassion and show it in action;
- share in the joy of discovering a sense of self-worth in God;
- substitute peace for pain and offer forgiveness as a way of dealing with hatred, hurt and suffering;
- stay patient when people let each other down or take their time about decisions, direction and doubts;
- seek kindness and respect for others, treating them as they would want to be treated, loving neighbours and living with enemies;
- show goodness and discover what it means to live a life of integrity;
- stand faithfully, side by side with people both in the good times when it's easy and the bad times when it's hard, showing commitment to God and community;
- serve with gentleness, understanding the importance of developing trust, valuing relationships with people and with God through humility and service;
- stop and show self-control, finding new ways of coping under the pressure to act and be a certain way, being honest about the difficulties of living together.

How does this compare with your group? *Express Community* is about sensitively demonstrating that, Jesus being our King, as members of his kingdom, God's values for life are important and beneficial to us and will therefore be both important and beneficial to our community. Of course all of the above can be found in Jesus, but they need also to be first found in us before they may be found in the people with whom we work, rest and play. Not that we should wait until we have achieved this before doing anything within community: we will never reach such perfection, but we should strive to demonstrate these values.

EXPRESS EXPERIENCE

A member of Tearfund's UK and Ireland Team recalls how three groups he was facilitating resorted to looking at their own 'fitness' rather than seeking ways of expressing their faith within community. He comments how interesting it was that 'it always happened at the point when [he] was challenging them to think about how they would begin to connect with their community. Fundamentally some of them did not want to do it so they tried to get back to the "comfort" of navel-gazing'.

The challenge is to seek ways of drawing the group of Christians you lead into the community in which they are seeking to live and serve. Real justice is about achieving your potential God's way, restoring his balance through justice, mercy and humility. The following sessions are designed to expand on these issues with your group.

SESSION 4

JUSTICE

Aim: To explore how restoring a sense of justice to our day-to-day life relates to God's call to express community.

YOU WILL NEED:

a Bible, a selection of objects of different sizes and weights for the Prize Pile, bathroom scales, Post-it notes, pens, A5 blank paper or flip chart paper.

Just hold on a minute! (20 mins)

Split your group into teams. The object of the game is for each team to try and hold as many objects as they can for as long as they can whilst they answer questions to earn more. Correct answers earn extra objects from the Prize Pile you have provided. Incorrect answers allow the opposing team the chance to steal or take one from the Prize Pile. Dropped objects return to the Prize Pile. Each team can either nominate one person to hold the objects or you could make it tougher and get them to hand over the objects to another team member after each question. Alternatively turn it into a relay race where they take the objects with them and then pass them on. You have a choice about how personal you want to make your questions.

A. NATIONAL

Your questions could include:

1. What's the average pocket money per week for an 11 to 16-year-old from Scotland?
     a) £7.75   b) £11.75   c) **£17.75**

2. The average monthly income of a 15 to 24-year-old is £726; how much do they spend on non-essentials?
     a) £145   b) **£245**   c) £345

3. What percentage of 13 to 16s buy their own music?
     a) **71%**   b) 73%   c) 75%

4. What percentage of 11 to 12s have a TV in their room?
     a) 72%   b) **82%**   c) 92%

5. What percentage of 16 to 19s own a mobile phone?
     a) 71%   b) 82%   c) **93%**

6. 51% of boys aged 11 to 16 will only wear branded clothes; what is the percentage for girls?

    a) **41%**   b) 52%   c) 63%

Answers are in **bold**. *Sources: Alliance and Leicester Cash Usage Survey, 2002; ROAR, 2002; NOP Survey, August 2002. SMRC Childwise Ltd, 2001. Young People and ICT DFES, 2001.*

B. LOCAL

Find questions about local news or issues. Get hold of local newspapers, hand them to each team and ask random questions such as: 'What's on special offer this week at Bert's Bakery?' or 'Turn to p.5 and find out who won "Best in Show" for their marigolds at this year's flower festival?' and so on. The first group to find the article, tear it out and bring it to the leader wins and gets to choose an object from the Prize Pile.

At the end of the game bring out a set of bathroom scales and weigh the objects (the winners are the team with the heaviest items, not the most – but do not tell them this until the end!) Alternatively, make a seesaw, pile up the objects and see who's won:

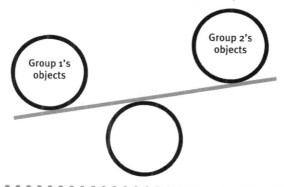

Just measuring? (10 mins)

Many of us see it as our aim in life to cram in as many possessions or experiences as we can – that is how we judge our success. Try and get hold of a traditional set of scales and explain that, as opposed to measuring only our successes, scales are often used as a sign of justice because they are designed to measure equality and create balance. The problem with using one set of scales to weigh up our success is that they do not offer anything to measure our actions against. Our natural tendency is to focus on ourselves, fill our lives with as many things as possible and hope it will make us happy. However it just makes us so self-absorbed that we:

- forget to consider how our decisions may affect others
- feel worthless because we have so much and still do not feel good, and
- feel worthless, believing that compared to others we've got nothing

Sometimes less is best, particularly if either the quality is greater, it's more beneficial to others or, for the purpose of this game, it's heavier.

Just you and me (10 mins)

Give each member of your group a piece of paper and ask them to write a list of their most treasured possessions.

Jesus said that 'a man's life does not consist in the abundance of his possessions' (Lk. 12:15). Explain that despite what Jesus says, most of us do find our identity in the things we own. Now hand each person a pile of Post-it notes.

Write one complimentary word on each of your Post-its to describe a characteristic you value about each of your fellow group members in turn and then stick it on their back.

Play a piece of background music. At the end of the music or when everyone has finished ask them to take the words off their backs and compare them with the list they made earlier. Explain that this is who they are! Ask how they think they can use their lives to grow into God's purposes rather than to gather possessions.

• •

Just us or just God? (20 mins)

What does the Bible have to say about 'just' living? Ask individuals to read through Isaiah 58 and pick out all the negative words (writing them down on the left-hand side of a piece of paper) and then read it again, this time trying to find contrasting positive words to write down on the right-hand side. For example:

rebellion, forsaken	seek, eager, know, near
exploit	acceptable, share, spend, honour
quarrelling, striking, malicious	humble, bowing
wicked	right
fast, hungry	food, feast
chains	loose, untie, free, break
injustice	just
oppressed	healing, help
naked	clothe
call, cry	noticed, heard, answer
darkness, night	day, light
poor	provide
wanderer	shelter, guide
needs	satisfy, joy

Alternatively, before the session, write each of the key words out yourself on separate pieces of card, place them face down and ask each member of your group to turn over two of them and try and find matching opposite pairs – you can use this as an opportunity to debate as a group whether you feel the pairs match or not and why. Alternatively, simply place the positive words in one box and the negative in another, count them up and see whether there's a balance.

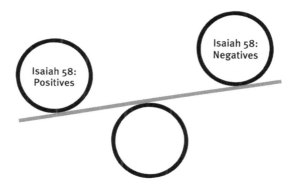

* *

A just balance (10 mins)

Just like scales of justice, God's mission is to restore balance to this world. Although Isaiah 58 is full of negative words it is encouraging that God regularly offers a positive match that will restore balance and inequality. Positives would only happen if Israel was prepared to adjust its actions, and will only happen in our community if we take the same attitude. The easiest way to start is to redress our lives in our community. Where there is oppression, he wants to bring freedom; where there is persecution, he wants to bring shelter and asylum, etc. He calls us to be part of his journey to restore a just balance.

1) Read out Isaiah 58 again, particularly verses 1-12. What words would you use to describe the kind of life God may be calling you to?

2) God wants a *just life* that is fair, right, impartial, honest, honourable, righteous, moral and truthful. He wants a just life that is simple, plain but effective. What practical things can we do to live a just life that will help to restore God's justice to his world?

3) Divide into three groups, hand each group a section from Isaiah and ask them to discuss it and come up with three suggestions for how they can *pray*, *act* and *live* more justly. Check out some of these ideas.

Just pray

Isaiah 58:3-5. God questions Israel's integrity. They prayed one thing and did the opposite but could not understand why their prayers did not get answered. List some of the injustices in your community and think of some simple but effective tips for just praying.

1) How do we make sure we pray with integrity? What things in your life do not disappear by simply shutting your eyes to pray?

2) Are there issues you are aware of that are causing injustice for others?

3) What things can we do to ensure we pray effectively and practically?

• •

Just act

Isaiah 58:6-7. God calls for some radical action to change the way people are treated, to give them what they need and deserve. Discuss some ideas for some simple but effective tips for taking action.

1) What sort of things do you have that others do not?

2) What things in your community are you aware of that make you angry?

3) What things in your community are you aware of that make you happy?

• •

Just live

Isaiah 58:10-12. Primarily God wants long-term efforts – a life spent for the sake of others. To be a repairer or restorer takes time and commitment. Discuss some ideas for some simple but effective tips for just living.

1) How might you make a change to your life to bring change to others?

2) How can you become a repairer of walls and a restorer of streets?

3) List some of the things you do or go to each day/week – how can you be just there? What tips could you think of for being different in the everyday stuff?

SESSION 5

MERCY

Aim: To understand the needs within our communities and how poverty develops. To engage with God's heart for those in need, his plans to reverse their fortunes and think about where we may fit in.

YOU WILL NEED:

Bible, masking tape or string, copies of ' *So what do you do?*' cards

Pull yourself together! (5 mins)

For many, the problems of those in need within our community are seen as being of their own making. Discuss this with the group.

'If only they would discipline their children better.'

'If only they would eat a healthier diet.'

'If only they were prepared to look for work.'

'If only they would take better care of their money.'

But do those views explain the whole story? What is it actually like to be constantly battling against the odds? The following role-play should help people to understand more clearly.

• •

So what would you do? (20 mins)

If you have a small group, ask them to sit in a circle and place yourself as leader in front of them on a 'hot seat'. If it is a larger group, split into smaller groups with someone taking the leader role within each group. Well in advance of this session take time to choose the leader roles carefully. Ensure they are comfortable with the exercise. Give leaders, including yourself, time to prepare possible answers for the group's responses to the scenarios.

Explain to the group/s that they will be asked to step into a person's shoes and respond to certain situations. Describe the scene (see the examples given overleaf and on page 65). Ask the group to discuss the situation and decide on a response. Use the question: 'So what do you do?' The group must answer what action they would take. Describe the scene a little bit more according to the direction the group have chosen and again ask: 'So what do you do?' The group responds again. Continue to describe the scene still further. This continues, with you responding increasingly quickly and placing more and more pressure on the group for a speedy response. The exercise finishes when in sheer desperation you either give up or the group cannot find a resolution to the problem. After each role-play, check individuals are OK and give them time to come out of the roles.

An example:

Scene 1

You are a single mum. You return to your high-rise flat and discover that your nine-year-old son, who should have let himself in, is not there. So what do you do?

Group: Wait for a few minutes to see if he turns up.
Leader: After 20 minutes he still has not shown up. So what do you do?
Group: Phone a friend's home to see if he's there.
Leader: Your phone has been cut off. So what do you do?
Group: Go out and look for him.
Leader: So where do you go?
Group: Go to his friend's house.
Leader: You get to his friend's house and discover that not only is he not there, but neither is his friend. The mother thought you were looking after them both, and starts shouting at you for not looking after her kid. So what do you do?
Group: Walk away and go to the school to see if they know where he is.
Leader: The school looks at their records and tell you that he hasn't been in school for the last couple of days. So what do you do?
Group: Go to the place where he normally hangs out.
Leader: You go to the local park and find him hanging out with some bigger lads. So what do you do?
Group: I tell him to come home with me.
Leader: He swears at you, impressing his friends. So what do you do?
Group: I grab hold of him and pull him back home.
Leader: Before you can get hold of him he runs off. It's getting dark. So what do you do now?
Group: I go to the police and ask them to help find my son and bring him home.
Leader: The police say they will do their best, but are already dealing with a number of emergency call-outs as you speak. They don't offer any chance of looking for him tonight. So what do you do?
Group: I go home and wait for him to come in.
Leader: It's nine o'clock and he still hasn't come home. So what do you do? etc.

• •

So how did it feel? (10 mins)

Having gone through the exercise using the different case studies, lead a discussion asking the following questions:

1. How did you feel during the exercise?

2. What impact would such a situation, if repeated on a daily basis, have on you mentally, socially, physically, spiritually?

3. If you were in that situation, how would you react to people who said that your problem was all your own fault?

4. How does this exercise help you to understand the issues facing those in need in your community?

• •

Glass houses (25 mins)

Look together at John 8:1-11. Depending upon the size of your group you may want to split down into groups of less than 10.

1. Read the passage twice.

2. The first time read it quickly, but stop after each situation, e.g. the ends of verses 3a, 4, 5, 7, 8, 9 and 11. Ask the group, 'So what would *you* do?' Wait for their answer – either get them to shout it out or write it down – then move on.

3. The second time you read it, take time and then ask the following questions:

   a. How did Jesus treat the teachers of the law and the Pharisees trying to condemn the woman?

   b. How was his response consistent with other teaching? (e.g. see Mt. 5:27-30 and Mt. 7:1-5).

   c. How does Jesus' example apply to the way we view the actions of others in our community?

   d. What was Jesus' attitude towards the woman?

   e. How do you think she would have responded to Jesus' words to her?

   f. How do you respond to a God who says those words to you? How does it change the way you view others?

• •

Neither do I condemn (5 mins)

For us to be able to help people in need in our communities, we need to be slower to judge and more willing to try to understand. Greater understanding will make mercy easier. It is justice that we aim to bring to our communities not judgement. Unlike many of his contemporaries, Jesus' brand of justice offered compassion rather than condemnation. In John 8:1-11, we see how Jesus challenged the Pharisees to look at their own lives before judging the life of the woman caught in adultery. If we are to have any impact on people's lives then we too have to do more than disturb the surface by throwing accusations. Bringing peace to their difficult situation will only happen through the grace and mercy found in the depths of forgiveness.

Forgive – never! (15 mins)

Mark out a line on the floor. Write 'Easy' at one end and 'Hard' at the other. Show your group the following questions and ask them to stand along the line according to their willingness to forgive.

1. Your best friend pinched your boy/girlfriend.

2. Your sister took your last packet of chewing gum.

3. Your mate ruined your designer sunglasses.

4. Your dog ate your homework.

5. Your best mate failed to pick you for their team.

6. Everybody got invited to a party but you.

7. Your little brother ruined the cardigan your auntie bought you.

• •

Five ways to find forgiveness (10 mins)

Use the following verses to offer suggestions why we should forgive, even when it's hard. Encourage people to get into pairs to discuss each situation, applying them to personal experiences if they can.

1. We all make mistakes (Jn. 8:7). *We've all got faults. You never know, the person you won't forgive today may be the person you're asking for forgiveness tomorrow.*

Discuss an occasion when you have refused to forgive someone and then needed his or her forgiveness soon afterwards.

2. They do not know any better (Lk. 23:34). *If Jesus can forgive the people that put him to death, surely we can forgive people who upset us without understanding the significance of their actions.*

Discuss times when you've been hurt through people doing something unintentionally.

3. It's not worth it (Gal. 5:14-15). *We need to regain a godly perspective on what is important and what is not. What's worth falling out over? Bearing grudges more often than not damages us more than the other person!*

How often have you fallen out over something, but cannot remember what the something was?

4. All within God's plan (Gen. 50:20). *If we believe that God loves us more than anything, then it's important that we trust him and understand that although our circumstances may change, his love never does.*

Have you ever seen good come out of a disastrous situation?

5. God forgives us (1 Jn. 1:9). *The greatest incentive to forgive is the fact that we have been forgiven so much by God. It is people who really know what it is to be forgiven that are most prepared to forgive.*

Reflect for a while on the ways in which God has forgiven you.

• •

At the end of the day

Do not let the sun go down while you are still angry (Eph. 4:26-27).

Allow time to reflect on any outstanding issues your group may need to sort out.

RESOURCES

SO WHAT DO WE DO?

Scene 1

You are a single mum. You return to your high-rise flat and discover that your nine-year-old son, who should have let himself in, is not there. So what do you do?

Scene 2

You are a 16-year-old girl. Your stepfather is abusive and violent at home. You are not doing well at school. One night your stepfather lashes out at you … it's getting too much. So what do you do?

Scene 3

You are on income support. You have a young family. Your child needs a new pair of shoes. So what do you do?

Scene 4

It's a Friday night in the middle of winter. You return to your bed-sit to discover that your electricity has run out and you have no spare meter-card. You do not have a job and your next giro is not due until next week. So what do you do?

SESSION 6

HUMILITY

Aim: To encourage the group to explore and experience the close relationship between humility and serving and to discover how true humility only comes from an understanding of God's view of his people.

YOU WILL NEED:

Bibles, a selection of wrapped boiled sweets, A5 pieces of card (some with humble words copied on them, others which are blank), music

Sweet feet (10 mins)

The aim of this game is to experience what it means to serve others and to be served by others.

In pairs, sit facing each other and attempt to feed your partner as many sweets with your bare feet as you can in two minutes.

Swap over after round one to allow each person the chance of serving and being served. You may want to provide wet-wipes, just in case some of your group have not washed for a few days!

Who got the most sweets? Whose feet smell?

• •

Humility is ... (20 mins)

Humility is more than kind words or sincere thoughts – it's about action! Highlight this point by encouraging your group to think about the active nature of being humble – what it actually means in practice. Copy the following onto individual cards, show the whole group, divide into smaller groups and then ask them to select one and construct a human sculpture, i.e. using your bodies to form a shape, structure or statement that demonstrates what it would mean to be:

humble, modest, poor, serving, meek, lowly, respectful, obliging, ordinary, inconspicuous, simple, submissive, gentle, mild, kind, helpful, considerate, polite, willing, cooperative, etc.

It is important that whatever we choose to do in community, we build in humility. Our motives need to come out of a sense of humility and our actions need to show it.

What did Jesus do? (20 mins)

Select some or all of the following verses and display them clearly around the room. Encourage the group, individually or in pairs, to spend time reflecting on each verse and to try to find as many specific things that Jesus did which show how humble he was.

Matthew 19:13-15	Jesus welcomes the children
Matthew 20:29-34	Jesus mixes with the beggars
Mark 1:40-41	Jesus meets with the sick
John 8:7-11	Jesus defends the woman
John 13:4	Jesus serves his friends

Provide blank pieces of card to record these actions for use later in the session. Try and create a reflective, thought-provoking atmosphere. You might want to select suitable background music that focuses on giving, serving, putting others first, etc. Bring the group together and get them to share what they have found.

Humble example (2 mins)

Being a humble Christian does not mean you are soft or a wimp. Do not let people walk all over you, using your good nature as a doormat. Humility is often seen as a sign of weakness but you only have to look at the descriptions of Moses in Numbers 12:3 and Jesus in Matthew 11:29 to realise that is not true. To be humble you have to be hard! Jesus acted in humility, knowing that it would bring him into conflict with society, involve criticism, abuse, self-denial, sacrifice, and eventually cost him his life (not the catchiest youth culture slogans you've ever heard!). His way of life came from a willingness to see injustice and to act against it, not in arrogance but with a 'God-confidence' about what he was doing. The essence of Moses' and Jesus' humility is their submission to God's will. They could be very strong in what they did because they knew that they were doing what God wanted them to do.

In communion (20 mins)

Why was Jesus able to live the way he did, and how can we develop a heart for our community like his?

Read John 13:1-17 together, focusing in particular on the way Jesus showed his disciples 'the full extent of his love' (v. 1). How did his passion for communion, i.e. unity and relationship, with his Father and his disciples enable him to serve in humility?

1. Upward: humility through communion with God (v. 3)

If anyone could be excused from being humble it would be Jesus. He knew he had all the power and glory (v. 3), and yet only ever used them to further God's name and not his own fame. When faced with death, the toughest decision of his life, Jesus proves his humility before God as he chooses to do God's will rather than his own (Mt. 26:36-45). This is only possible because he is confident of God's will for his life. He only knows God's will for his life because he has lived in constant communion with his Father, developing a deep relationship with him.

DISCUSSION POINTERS:

- What kind of things do you feel you need to make a priority of in your life in order to ensure that you have the same sort of God-confidence that Jesus had?
- As you seek to be humble towards your community, how can you ensure you know God's will for your life?
- In what ways might you develop a deeper relationship with God?

2. Inward: humility through communion with each other (v. 14)

Not only does Jesus serve us as individuals, but he calls us to serve each other in humility too. Everything we do should seek to put God on a pedestal. If our focus ever shifts from him to us we'll soon go astray! It is God who hands out any talents that our lives display. We need to avoid getting big-headed, arrogant, selfish or thinking of ourselves more highly than we ought (Phil. 2:3).

DISCUSSION POINTERS:

- How do you feel about Jesus' command to 'wash one another's feet' (v. 14)? In what other ways might you serve your fellow group members?
- In what ways might it be easier to remain humble within a group setting as opposed to being alone
- What structures might you need to put in place to ensure you remain humble in your attitudes towards one another? (such as fostering an environment in which people feel free to correct and challenge one another)?

3. Outward: humility through communion with others (v. 15)

If you struggle to serve each other, how do you expect to serve your community? When faced with all that need, did Jesus ever wonder, 'are these people worth putting myself out for?' Not putting his own needs and comforts before anyone else, Jesus naturally gave people his time and effort; any needs of theirs were greater than any of his own (Phil. 2:4). Sometimes Jesus did walk away, sometimes he needed his own space. There is a need for some balance. This is why discerning God's will for each situation through prayer is crucial. We still face many situations that are the same as those which Jesus faced two thousand years ago: we have all passed the guy in the street selling *The Big Issue*; we all know ill people; we see children hurting through broken homes; we know of oppressed women – but what do we do?

DISCUSSION POINTERS:

- Verse 15 talks about doing 'as I have done for you'. Jesus may be talking about serving him in return. If so, in what ways can we serve God in the same ways he was prepared to serve us?

- Jesus may also be talking about following his example and serving others. If this is the case, in what way do you feel ready to serve others?

- In what way do you not feel ready to serve others? What might help you to overcome this?

- What might be the potential difficulties of your community accepting your acts of service? People may not be thrilled when you offer to serve them: what can you do about this?

What if? (20 mins)

We need to see ourselves, and the people around us, through God's eyes – what does he feel for them and me? If our hearts were able to feel even a hint of the emotion God feels for his hurting people, I doubt we could do anything other than act on their behalf in the ways Jesus did. Now may be an appropriate point to challenge your group about how humble they are in their everyday lives. Ask your group to find a place to relax, perhaps play a suitable piece of music, and read out the mediation below. At some point, possibly at the end, it might be appropriate to invite members of your group to take the cards from the two exercises earlier and select one they feel they need to ask God for more help with, whether in relation to the value they place on him, themselves or others.

WHAT IF, FOR ONE DAY, JESUS WERE TO BECOME YOU?

What if, for twenty-four hours, Jesus wakes up in your bed, walks in your shoes, lives in your house, assumes your schedule? Your boss becomes his boss, your mother becomes his mother, your pains become his pains? With one exception, nothing about your life changes. Your health does not change. Your circumstances do not change. Your schedule is not altered. Your problems are not solved. Only one change occurs.

What if, for one day and one night, Jesus lives your life with his heart? Your heart gets the day off, and your life is led by the heart of Christ. His priorities govern your actions. His passions drive your decisions. His love directs your behavior.

What would you be like? Would people notice a change? Your family – would they see something new? Your co-workers – would they sense a difference? What about the less fortunate? Would you treat them the same? And your friends? Would they detect more joy? How about your enemies? Would they receive more mercy from Christ's heart than from yours?

And you? How would you feel? What alterations would this transplant have on your stress level? Your mood swings? Your temper? Would you sleep better? Would you see sunsets differently? Death differently? Taxes differently? Any chance you'd need fewer aspirin or sedatives? How about your reaction to traffic delays? (Ouch, that touched a nerve!) Would you still dread what you are dreading? Better yet, would you still do what you are doing?

Would you still do what you had planned to do for the next twenty-four hours? Pause and think about your schedule. Obligations. Engagements. Outings. Appointments. With Jesus taking over your heart, would anything change?

Keep working on this for a moment. Adjust the lens of your imagination until you have a clear picture of Jesus leading your life, then snap the shutter and frame the image. What you see is what God wants. He wants you to 'think and act like Christ Jesus' (Phil. 2:5).

God's plan for you is nothing short of a new heart. If you were a car, God would want control of your engine. If you were a computer, God would claim the software and the hard drive. If you were an airplane, he'd take his seat in the cockpit. But you are a person, so God wants to change your heart.

'But you were taught to be made new in your hearts, to become a new person. That new person is made to be like God – made to be truly good and holy' (Eph. 4:23–24).

God wants you to be just like Jesus. He wants you to have a heart like his. I'm going to risk something here. It's dangerous to sum up grand truths in one statement, but I'm going to try. If a sentence or two could capture God's desire for each of us, it might read like this:

God loves you just the way you are, but he refuses to leave you that way. He wants you to be just like Jesus.[7]

Closing thought …

Being Christian does not mean we are better than others; it just means we have accepted God's willingness to suffer the consequences of our past and admitted we need his help for the future. The lengths someone is prepared to go to for the benefit of another is a good way to measure a person's humility. However we must be careful, because some of the greatest deeds often go unseen. In seeking to be humble through acts of compassion, we have to be careful that as our hands turn to the needs of others, we do not forget to deal with issues in our own life that God's pointing out as areas for change. To show humility even when nobody is looking is truly a sign of a humble person.

EXPRESS TOGETHER

So if this is what God requires, why do not we live this way? Maybe it is because we are not aware of the needs of the people with whom we share our community. How do we act justly if we do not know the injustice? How do we show mercy when we're not aware of those without mercy? How can we walk humbly if we do not know who needs serving?

OBJECTIVE CONNECTING

A good way to start becoming more aware of your community is to gather as much local information as you can. Facts and statistics about your community will be invaluable as you progress through the Express Community process. Greater knowledge is also a good way of winning over those who may initially be sceptical about the issue. Get your group involved. Share out the tasks and then bring what has been found to the whole group when you meet again. If members of your group have expressed some fear at the thought of connecting with their community face to face, this is a good way to start getting people involved in the process. You might of course decide to do this research as a group: see it as a kind of field trip or a good group-bonding exercise.

Finding the information

A visit to the local reference library is as a good a place to start as any. There are many more activities on assessing needs in Stage 2: Connecting within Community, but this is a good way to begin raising awareness of the local issues. Ask for help in finding out about the particular area or issue you are interested in, and a member of staff should be able to point you in the right direction. Sources of information will include:

- ward profiles
- county/borough profiles
- local authority departmental reports

What to look for

Do not be overwhelmed by the amount of statistics and information you find! Remember, your aim is not to write a PhD but to find out basic things about your area that will surprise and motivate other people in your group to take more seriously the issues in their community. What surprises you or makes you think is probably a good indication of what will make an impact on others too. The library should have a census, which contains detailed information about your local community.

Examples of things to look out for are the:

- number of elderly people living alone
- number of single parent families
- number of substandard accommodation units
- number of people living on or below the poverty line
- number of unemployed
- rate and nature of crime
- proportion of failing schools; plus any other categories specific to your own community

Other sources of information[8]

THE INTERNET

The internet is full of information about everything, anything and nothing. Connecting within community online can be quite time-consuming and expensive, so browse wisely and set yourself a limit on how long you are going to look for. You will find a lot of objective connecting can be done simply by logging on and browsing – which is great if members of your group are particularly into that kind of thing. Simply punch in the name of your community at www.upmystreet.com, or try www.statistics.gov.uk/neighbourhood.

EARLY YEARS DEVELOPMENT AND CHILDCARE PARTNERSHIP (LOCAL CHILDCARE PARTNERSHIPS IN SCOTLAND)

These bodies may have facts about the children living in your community. Log on to your favoured search engine and enter 'Early Years Development and Childcare

Partnership' followed by your region/community and you should be able to find the contact details or information for your area. Sure Start is also a useful place to look – www.surestart.gov.uk. This is a government programme that aims to achieve better outcomes for children, parents and communities by increasing the availability of childcare for all children, improving health, education and emotional development for young children and supporting parents in their aspirations towards employment.

INDICES OF DEPRIVATION

The Neighbourhood Renewal Unit has a record of the level of deprivation for every ward and local authority area in England. These are available online from the www.neighbourhood.gov.uk/indices.asp

LOCAL STATUTORY INFORMATION

Local statutory bodies, such as social services or the health authority, have masses of information about your community. Why not contact your local council, explain that you are researching the needs of your particular community, and ask them if they have any studies of your community which they feel would be relevant and whether you can have access to them?

LOCAL COUNCIL FOR VOLUNTARY SERVICE (CVS)

Your local CVS may be aware of other groups who have carried out recent surveys of your community. They may have access to any reports that were produced as a result, or at least know how you can get hold of them. Log on to www.nacvs.org.uk to find your local CVS.

POLICE

Contact your local or regional police and ask them what community problems they are aware of and whether they have crime statistics or crime prevention initiatives. Keep a record of who you contact; you may want to get in touch later on in the Express Community process once you have decided which area of action you feel called to focus on.

THE BESOM FOUNDATION

The Besom is a Christian charity based in South London. It helps people make a difference. It connects people who want to give money, time, skills, or things, with those who are in need. It ensures that what is given is used effectively. It is currently mainly operational only in London but centres are being established elsewhere in the country. The service it provides is free. Log on to www.besom.com for more information.

OTHER GROUPS

What other community initiatives are already in existence? What is their purpose? What issues and needs do they come across? Who runs them? What are other Christian groups doing in the area? Are there groups that could benefit from additional support? Are there significant needs that no group seems to be meeting at present?

Presenting the information

Be creative: a list of statistics can sometimes seem very dry. Here are just a few ideas:

1. To highlight a statistic, get a proportion of the group to stand up to reflect the proportion of the local area that are unemployed, homeless, etc. For example, if there is 25 per cent unemployment in the area, get a quarter of the group to stand up.

2. Hold a quiz under the title 'How well do you know your community?' Intersperse questions of local history and local geography with questions to do with local need. Check to see how different their answers are from the real answers.

3. Put eye-catching posters up around the room giving quotes or statistics. (Write the source of information on the poster so that people know where the statement comes from.)

4. Give the youth group the statistics and ask them to act out in a church service a drama based on the information.

Conclusion

This research will give you an insight into some of the issues in your local area. However, statistics can only give a limited, and sometimes misleading, view of complex personal situations. Activities that will provide a more personal insight into areas and issues of need can be found throughout Chapters 3 and 4.

[1] Max Lucado, *Just Like Jesus* (Nashville, TN: Word Publishing, 1998), p. 3.

[2] DFID, *Making Globalisation Work for the World's Poor. An Introduction to the UK Government's White Paper on International Development* (London: DFID, 2000), pp. 2-3. These statistics represent revised figures based on two World Bank reports: *World Development Indicators 2003* and *Global Economic Prospects 2004*.

[3] UNESCO. EFA Global Monitoring Report 2004.

[4] The Fairtrade Foundation, which was set up by major development agencies in 1992, launched an independent Fairtrade Mark in 1994. This mark guarantees that people producing the food we buy are guaranteed a fair wage and that they and their environment will be treated with respect.

[5] Shelter, *Coming in from the Cold. Progress Report on the Government's Strategy on Rough Sleeping* (Shelter, Rough Sleepers Unit, August 2000).

[6] *Star Wars: Episode I: The Phantom Menace*. Lucasfilm Ltd, 2000.

[7] Reprinted by permission. Max Lucado, *Just Like Jesus* (Nashville, TN: Word Publishing, 1998). All rights reserved.

[8] Adapted from S. Chalke, *Faithworks Unpacked 3* (Eastbourne: Kingsway, 2002), pp. 49-50.

STAGE 2

CONNECTING
WITHIN
COMMUNITY

The purposes of a man's heart are **deep waters,** but a man of **understanding** draws them out (Prov. 20:5).

Chapter 3

LOOK, STOP, NOW LISTEN!

Stage Two, Connecting within Community, is about understanding the complexities of God's character, whilst at the same time unravelling the concerns of your community. This is one of the greatest, but most rewarding, challenges of *Express Community*. Your ability to listen both to your God and to your community will be crucial in the formation of your concept of integral mission. As a follower of God's life, the images of him you have will speak volumes to the people you meet. So too, as followers of local life, these people will carry images of community which will be invaluable to you. You should have already started to take some steps towards Connecting within Community as a result of some initial objective research at the end of Stage One. However don't think that having been equipped with some basic facts you can jump ahead to the next stage. As you recap the facts you do know, you may be feeling confident and optimistic, but you should understand at this juncture that there is still much to learn. Progress in life is not always as straightforward as we might like. Just when we think we've got it cracked a challenge will come along to crumble our pride. Numerous expeditions across the Artic and voyages across the Atlantic have ended prematurely because of a failure fully to appreciate the depth of understanding that was required to negotiate the task ahead.

Objective research alone will not be enough to complete *Express Community*, but it does serve as a useful guideline as you begin to weigh up what you've found so far against what you are about to discover as a result of Stage Two: Connecting within Community. Subjective research, that is, what people actually think and feel, is the key to deepening your understanding of what causes really lie beneath some of the more obvious issues that by now are beginning to surface as a result of your initial crack at connecting within your community. In order to express community it will be essential that you do everything in your power and in God's power to find out what makes your community tick, what makes it tough and in particular what thoughts the people have about ways to turn it around. As you begin to face up to the issues that may be submerged deep within your community it is inevitable that you will encounter all kinds of challenges. The more you connect the more they will come to the surface, and the more you will be called to face them head on. It may be that beneath the surface lurks at least another two thirds of relatively uncharted territory which, should you choose to ignore during this stage, could be your downfall later in the process.

Try to see all your research as the means of completing a fuller picture of what causes concern in your community. Rather than obstacles preventing progress it may be better to view challenges as opportunities from which it will be necessary to promote some kind of change. On meeting Jesus people are generally left with three challenges, either to retreat from him, to skirt around him or to work through him. How you and your community respond to challenges will determine how well you progress together. Providing you are committed to get through any initial difficulties, you will soon begin to understand what it means truly to express community. Your ability to connect with your community will be determined by how able you are to take the chances God offers you, channel the energy the Spirit gives you, and change as a response to the challenges Jesus leads you through as group, as community and in your personal life. Are you ready for this?

When you finally conquer Stage Two and approach Stage Three, you will need to use all your research to inform your strategy and plans for Acting within Community. For this to happen it will be crucial for you to have connected to your full potential here. Simply citing a lack of knowledge or ignorance, as a result of shallow research now, will never make up for choosing the wrong move then. Like any note of absence, though it may temporarily excuse your actions, nothing will change the fact that at some point during the proceedings you have not fully taken part, and consequently have failed to do what is required of you. You will either be forever playing catch up, or worse still, you will have missed so much schooling that it will be impossible for you ever to join in again.

Taking time to stop, look and listen as you begin to go out and touch the lives of real people with real needs will help to clarify the vision of what God wants to see happen in your community. In Matthew 9:35-37 it is Jesus' ability to see through the crowd to the individuals that form it, that enables his heart to be filled with a deep compassion for their situation. The only way for you to feel this is to come face to face with people who form the community with which you are attempting to connect. Going to where people are will undoubtedly give you more data for your research; it will even help you to sieve through some of the objective research you have already gathered; but most of all, as you begin to draw alongside some of the pains, hurts and sometimes joys which exist all around you, it will begin to change you. The session plans within this chapter will give you simple but effective steps to begin to meet with and listen to the people in your community.

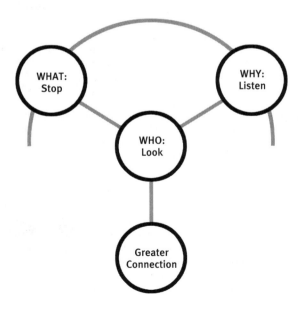

THE CHANCE OF LOOKING

Even if the time spent assessing the issues confirms what you already thought, it will give you greater confidence to move on, and will give other people and groups greater confidence to support the work you do. There are few things more demotivating than finding, a year down the road, that you have missed the mark. Giving time to identifying the issues and assessing the extent of the needs in your community will increase your chances of doing something of worth in the future. Looking before you leap will help you to use all that God has given you to the full. When Nehemiah returned to the crumbling ruins of Jerusalem (Neh. 2:11-16), he must have been sorely tempted to just jump in and get straight on with what God had called him to do – the rebuilding of the walls. After all, the need as he rode into the city could not have been more obvious. Yet, as Kidner points out, 'For all his speed and drive, he does not rush into action or into talk';[1] his first act was to investigate the walls, assessing the need. He looked before he leapt!

It is not always easy to hit your target, especially when you are involved in a process by which you are only slowly becoming aware of the facts, but as yet don't have all of them. Listening is tough – even tougher when there are so many distractions. Have you ever tried that exercise where you sit back to back with a partner, one of you with a blank piece of paper and a pencil and the other with a drawing of an object, and have one of you attempt to describe the object without saying what it is, while the other draws? As if that isn't difficult enough, occasionally some twisted facilitator will get you to do it whilst sitting alongside a whole load of other people. The dilemma is that the more you begin to hear and understand about your community, the more you begin to build a picture of what things might look like if only you started to do something. You start to guess what you might hear or see next and choose to take action. The danger of even considering trying to meet needs at this stage is that you will end up producing something wholly inappropriate, spreading yourself too thinly; and at the same time increasing the risk of damaging any chances you have of completing the Express Community process. You might find that as well as failing to meet the needs of your community, you fail to meet the needs of your group. Then where do you go? It is better to wait until you are sure about what, when and how you can contribute to your community before thinking about acting on your research. Try the exercise above with your group and see how good they are at listening! Road signs work well for this game and you can find hundreds in the Highway Code!

THE CHALLENGE OF STOPPING

As you build momentum entering this second stage of *Express Community*, being prepared to keep stopping will be hard to do. Some people in your group may feel frustrated at the thought of spending more time connecting with their local community in identifying areas of real need. Some may even feel uncomfortable at the thought of spending any time at all. You may find voices of disapproval begin to surface: 'Why bother when all the needs are so obvious anyway: unemployment, bad housing, youth out of control, dangerous roads ... ?' or worse still, 'Why bother to ask the local community what they think when surely our group will have a better understanding of the issues from a Christian perspective?'

Do not allow these kinds of comments and the fear that they might damage the morale of the rest of your group to push you into a commitment for which you are not ready. It is important that you take these comments on board – you may even agree with some of them. Nevertheless a decision to take the time to listen to your community has to be made because everyone wants to, not because you feel you have to. If you don't stop to listen, you will never really connect with your community. It is the fundamental basis of developing a relationship with individuals and groups in the community. This cannot be stressed enough. It may take some members of your group longer to realise this than others. Reacting against seemingly negative comments will not help this happen.

HELPFUL HINT

Your group may benefit from an opportunity to discuss openly how they are feeling at the beginning of Stage Two of the Express Community process. To encourage this, try dividing your group into threes, handing each a sheet of road signs. After they have spent some time relaxing, trying to guess what each might mean, ask them to pick out signs that would best describe:

● how they are feeling after Stage One, and

● what they would hope to feel once they have listened to their community, and

● perhaps then finish with a time of prayer

Being honest about frustrations may help. It is hard sitting around waiting to discover what your next move might be, when you are used to seeing instant, ready-made solutions to situations you might be facing in your own lives. Connecting within Community will involve a certain amount of patience. The following drama illustrates the value of listening and the potentially tragic consequences if you do not.

LEARNING FROM LIFE

The doctor is sitting behind a desk writing some notes as another person, the patient, comes into the room with a bad limp and clearly in pain. The doctor looks up, sees the problem and immediately applies a bandage to the leg, whilst offering a few comforting words like, 'I'm sure you must have been in a lot of pain ... I know what it's like; having sore shins is terrible. This will do the trick. Let me know if you need any further help,' and so on. The patient looks surprised and a little upset, but every time she attempts to say something, the doctor interrupts with a phrase like, 'You'll be fine now.' In the end the patient gives up trying to talk to the doctor. The doctor finishes the bandaging and goes back to his desk looking very satisfied, mumbling something like, 'Close the door behind you as you leave' or 'Send the next person in if you would ...' As the patient leaves, looking very despondent, she suddenly clutches her heart and doubles up in pain.

THE CALL OF LISTENING

However drained Connecting within Community may leave you feeling, see it as a reminder of the need to build in times when you simply bathe in God's presence. Value the need to look continually for what he is doing and wants to do through you, your group and your community. When he knows you have had enough, he'll put you back on your feet, point you in the right direction and send you off on the course he has set for you all. The drama above illustrates perfectly the effects of jumping to conclusions about a situation and not being prepared to listen. Hopefully people won't die as a result of you not listening to your community but if you act according to either your agenda as leader or your group's agenda rather than the community's or God's, people may very well get hurt. Being well meaning is not enough. We need to listen to people if we are to discover their needs. You have probably experienced occasions when people have jumped to the wrong conclusion about you. How did that feel? Maybe you have jumped to the wrong conclusions about others? What would happen if your group jumped to the wrong conclusions about your community? Of course, the best doctors are the ones who spend time listening carefully to their patient's description of their symptoms before making a diagnosis.

Whatever facts you've discovered so far, when it comes truly to Connecting within Community, there is no substitute in being prepared for completely submerging yourself in the lives of the people around you, or at least as deeply as your current level of confidence will allow you to go. The way you choose to connect is just as key as the fact that you are connecting. It cannot be emphasised enough that *Express Community* is not some sort of survey of needs, which you'll take away to process in the comfort of your own home, forgetting everything you have heard, seen or done. It is about fully immersing yourself in the lives of the people who make up your community in order to find a better way to live with them to greater effect. This is the aim of *Express Community* after all: finding a way to an integral mission that involves Living within Community.

Are you prepared to walk out into your community and to leave your previous shallow assumptions behind you? You may find yourself overwhelmed by all kinds of feelings, ranging from confusion to compassion and conviction and complete and utter helplessness. At times it may feel like you're getting more and more out of your depth, but with each need you discover, you should find yourself increasingly filled with a sense of God's vision of, and for, his people. At times it may feel like you are being battered by never-ending waves of need both from your group and from your community; you may even find yourself knocked off your feet. You may find it hard at first to let your emotions flow, particularly as leader in front of your group, but don't panic. God knows how you are feeling; he feels it too. Do not be afraid of letting yourself go, stretch out your arms, and allow God's Holy Spirit to reveal his heart for your community. As he does so, you will begin to notice a difference in the way you view him, your group and your community.

CONTINUING CONNECTING

Stage Two of *Express Community* offers a relatively structured model of Connecting within Community, for the reasons outlined above. We recognise that at times you will need to be disciplined about your approach if you are to get the full benefit of this guide. It is hoped that your ultimate ability to express community will be more effective as a result of the methods, skills and the steps suggested at this stage. Connecting within Community is one of the key tasks of the whole process. Everything hinges on this stage: what you have reflected on so far and what you will choose to act upon later. Groups who have already worked with this material have found it a challenge, but those that have planned carefully and met regularly have achieved a great deal.

EXPRESS EXPERIENCE

A church in the heart of Liverpool spent a whole year talking to the community and discovering their needs. A door-to-door survey of community needs highlighted the need for:

- A playgroup and a provision for children. This now runs Monday to Friday with a staff of seven with a waiting list of children wanting to join the playgroup.

- A drop-in centre that local people could use. They decided to open up the coffee shop. It has now been in operation for more than 10 years

- There were a large number of children, particularly in the teenage bracket, who had been expelled or excluded from mainstream education. They decided to renovate the basement into a skills school and community centre.

Elaine Reece explains: 'Over time people have come to trust us and they've done that because they've seen what we are about. They've seen that we care for them and meet their needs right where they are.'

Stage Two is designed to help your group to listen to its community and, through doing so, begin to identify key issues and needs. In the drama discussed earlier, the doctor, in failing to listen to the patient, not only failed to diagnose the real problem but was also guilty of devaluing her. He treated the patient as a passive target of professional expertise rather than as a person. Likewise we will end up denying people respect and worth if we merely do things *for* them rather than *with* them. In fact, we may end up helping people to meet *our* needs rather than theirs, such as their meeting our need to feel needed or our desire to feel we are doing something worthwhile. Mrs Jones, a lady who has lived in poverty for most of her life, said in an article in a national newspaper: 'The poor are so often seen as the passive object of history rather than its active subjects ... poor people want to be included and not judged and "rescued" at times of crisis.'[2]

'Ownership', the feeling that we are listened to, that we are included, that we have a say, that we have some responsibility for an initiative, is crucially important for us all. It completely changes our outlook. However you choose to meet God in your personal devotion, your group devotion and your community devotion, what will be your reaction? Will you be prepared to stop and respect his challenge, look and reflect on the opportunities he gives you, listen and respond to his calling? To express community to any effect you are going to have to see the need to do all three – these are integral requirements of Stage Two: Connecting within Community as they are with the whole of the Express Community process. Missing any of the links of subjective research may well result in yet another failed connection, for you, your group, your community and your God.

KEY QUESTIONS

1. *Who* in your life, your group and your community do you imagine it will be difficult/easy to listen to?

2. *What* do you feel you know about your community already? What do you expect listening to them will achieve for you personally, your group, your community? What concerns or excites you about what lies ahead of you during this particular stage?

3. *Why* do you feel it is important to listen to your community? How would you summarise this in light of what you have just read? In what ways might you need to communicate this differently depending on whether you are communicating this to:

● your group?
● your community?
● your Christian community?

4. Finally, *how* will you ensure you build in the need to look, stop and listen to your group, your community, and your God? What may this mean you need to do throughout the *Express Community* process? The principles you establish now will determine what you do in the future.

Why not try the drama outlined above with your group and see how they respond? Ask them about the way the doctor has acted. What about the patient: how would they feel if they were treated like that? Would they ever go to that doctor again? What lessons does this teach you about the value of listening to your community?

ENGAGE YOUR GROUP
EASY-TO-USE SESSION PLANS

SKILLS AND TOOLS TRAINING FOR YOUR GROUP

You will need to decide what training your group will need to help them listen to their community and gather information. For example:

- Do they need help in developing their listening skills or knowing how to ask questions? See Session 8.

- Do they need training in using some of the various connection methods? See the connection tasters in Session 9. Having decided what training people will need, plan how that training can take place. Each of the following sessions should be used as a guide; you may want to use them in your existing group or as special workshops.

CHOOSING THE RIGHT METHODS

Questionnaires are often the first thing that comes to mind when people think of finding out the needs of their community. There is real skill in devising a questionnaire that asks questions in the most helpful way. They have many advantages, but to rely on them alone can give a misleading picture. You need to be sure that they will give you the information you require. Questionnaires may not always be the best way of listening to people, so have a good look at all the skills outlined in Session 9. The activities that follow will both explain the methods of connection, which are necessary to help your community to share, and also begin to develop in the group the skills required to employ them effectively. These can be used with:

- your group
- as many people as possible from within your wider Christian community
- friends, neighbours and others
- other groups, such as the local bowls team, dance or football club
- people outside your Christian community, such as councillors, the regeneration officer, or the youth offenders team

---

EXPRESS EXPERIENCE

A church from a conservative theological background with an elderly congregation was just beginning to explore ways in which it could become more involved in the community. Church members felt quite threatened by the idea of talking and listening to people. They lacked confidence in that environment. The idea of starting with people they knew and gradually working outwards was a real breakthrough for them. It meant that they could build confidence and get to the point where they were ready to listen to the views of outsiders.

Connection methods are a great way of raising levels of interest within the community and of digging deeper into the issues. Not all the methods will be appropriate to your situation but it is worth trying them out anyway, even if only on members of your group: you may be surprised by how much you learn through them. In Chapter 4 you will have the opportunity to decide which skills would be the most appropriate to be used with each of the individuals or groups you identify within your community. However, it is worth making a note of any thoughts that arise from this chapter too.

SESSION 7

LOOK

Aim: To help your group to look at their community from a different perspective as they take a fresh look during a walk.

YOU WILL NEED:

to plan a walk around your community: one route through your locality, between one and two miles long, for every four to five people in the group. Make each route as varied as possible, including shops, leafy lanes, housing estates and local parks. Ensure each group has at least one responsible adult with them. Each group will need a map with their route clearly marked.

HELPFUL HINT:

The nature of this session means it has the potential to take longer than you may usually allow for your sessions. Consider either selecting the most appropriate sections for your group, increasing your time together or spreading it over a few weeks.

Lasting impression (15 mins)

- As a large group, ask people to speak out those things that they think are *good* about the local area. Write these down on a large sheet of paper.

- Then ask people to speak out those things that they think are *bad* about the area. Again, write these things down on a large sheet of paper.

- Stick both sheets on the wall and leave them there to refer back to at the end of the session. Explain that the group will have a chance to check out how accurate their impression of their community is later in the session.

• •

Stop. Look! (2 mins)

We are often so used to our own environment that we take much for granted. We fail to see things that could tell us much about our area. This session is designed to help you slow down and take a fresh and more in-depth look at your local area.

You may want to reflect for a moment on Nehemiah 2:11-16. After being taken into exile, the Jews began to return to Jerusalem in 538 BC. Whilst the Babylonians had taken them far off, the Persians allowed them to resettle in their home towns.

Nehemiah received reports that Jerusalem's attempts to rebuild the walls were failing under opposition and returned to get things moving again. On his return he studied the walls to get to grips with the task ahead. What was required may have been obvious, but rather than jumping straight in, Nehemiah stopped, looked and thoroughly assessed the situation. A good model of community connection if ever there was one!

Explain to the group that they are going to go on a walk around the local area. They are to walk at a relaxed pace – no prizes for the group that finishes their route first! Just as Nehemiah walked the walls of Jerusalem examining the task that lay ahead of him in rebuilding the city, so a walk in our own community can begin to give us an understanding of the task that could lie ahead. As well as looking it will be important to *stop* and pray, both before you go and particularly during your walk. Ask God to reveal things more clearly, to open your eyes and your heart to the community as he sees it.

> **EXPRESS EXPERIENCE**
>
> Building in times of focused prayer at particular points or places during a walk is key to developing a new understanding of community. From personal experience, as a result of going out once, our group decided to spend the next six months praying and walking the area we felt God was calling us to focus on. Whilst at first we walked and prayed, soon we began meeting people who would quite naturally strike up conversations with us. Sometimes God's idea of expressing community is quite subtle, gentle and perhaps more natural than we first imagine.

Local life (45 mins)

Brainstorm some ideas about the best ways to ensure your group take everything in. Here are 10 tips for connecting with local life:

1. *Living* – Encourage them to think about what it's like to live in the different places they see: the big house, the old people's home, the housing estate. How old are the cars? How many do people have?

2. *Occupation* – Are there opportunities for people to be employed locally? If so, what are they?

3. *Construction* – Look at the buildings: are there factories, warehouses, derelict buildings, or houses that are boarded up? How old are they? Are they smart or neglected? How do you think this makes people feel?

4. *Amenities* – What about the shops? Go in and look. Buy something. What foods do they sell? How expensive are the goods? Do they take credit cards? What are the opening hours? Do they give the appearance of thriving or are they barely scraping by?

5. *Leisure* – What opportunities are there for relaxation and entertainment? What are the pubs like? What is the state of the local parks? Are these places that feel particularly welcoming or threatening?

6. *Litter* – Are the streets clean and well lit, or littered with tin cans, chewing gum and cigarette butts? Is there a feeling of pride in the area, or do you perceive a low morale? What messages of self-worth and value are being given to people by this environment?

7. *Individuals* – Encourage them to look at the people they see: who are they and what are they doing? What might they be feeling? How is their morale? What level of self-esteem do they seem to possess?

8. *Faith* – Note the variety and number of churches, mosques and synagogues.

9. *Education* – Are there any schools? What kind of schools are they? What condition are they in?

10. All the time consider the kind of words you would use if you were asked to describe the place to a stranger.

Stress to the group that these are just suggestions to start them off. They may think of many more. The key is for people to *stop, look, listen* and *talk* about what they see and hear. Remind them to stop occasionally and simply *pray* that God would reveal something new, or maybe that he would begin to intervene in situations or open up opportunities for you to begin to build relationships at this early stage in the process. Finally:

- Check to see if people are clear as to the purpose of the walk
- Get people into groups of four or five, and give each a map with the route of their walk on it
- Ask them to be back in 45 minutes (unless you are pushed for time)
- Spend a few moments praying together before you head off

● ●

Back 'home' (30 mins)

As the groups return, ask people to jot down on a piece of paper some of the feelings they experienced during the walk and the things they think they have learnt. Explain that they will have an opportunity to share with their small group in a few minutes. Once everyone has returned and had a few minutes to reflect, explain that each group should divide the area they walked through into sections. This could be by geographical area (e.g. King George's Avenue, Harold Estate, etc.) or by land use (e.g. shops, private housing, council housing, industrial estates, etc.). Ask the group to answer the following questions concerning each section of their walk:

- How did you feel during that section of the walk?
- What do you think it would be like to live in that area?
- What factors are working towards developing a sense of well-being?
- What factors are working against developing a sense of well-being?

Show and tell (15 mins)

Draw the groups back together. Ask each group to share just two things that particularly struck them from their walk and the discussion. You may want to highlight common themes and pull out key areas of learning, but at this stage it is just as important to simply pray about some of the issues that have been raised.

HELPFUL HINT:

Don't forget to keep all the notes to allow you to refer back to them later in the Express Community process.

SESSION 8

STOP: SKILLS FOR EFFECTIVE COMMUNITY CONNECTION

Aim: To develop your group's ability to listen more effectively. To understand how asking the right questions is key to discovering people's real needs.

YOU WILL NEED:

a Bible, paper, pens, questions about the local community

PART A: LISTENING SKILLS

Listening is a crucial skill to learn if you wish to understand and not misinterpret what people are saying. This first part of this session will look at verbal and non-verbal listening skills and potential barriers to listening. There will be a chance to practise new skills at the end of the session.

· ·

Are you listening? (15 mins)

Before the session, brief two people to act out a conversation about their last holiday, where one person is being a very bad listener – interrupting frequently, looking bored, fidgeting, and avoiding eye contact.

● Stop the interview after three or four minutes and ask the interviewee:
   a) how he or she knew that the interviewer wasn't listening; and
   b) how he or she felt about not being listened to.

● Then, as a whole group:
   a) list the qualities the listener was exhibiting;
   b) list any other factors that lead to bad listening.

● Write all this feedback on a large sheet of paper.

· ·

Learning a new language (10 mins)

Take the above exercise a stage further by asking the group to categorise their observation as either *poor verbal listening skills or poor non-verbal listening skills*.

Encourage the group to think of positive listening skills that might help to eliminate some of the points raised during their feedback, for example:

VERBAL LISTENING SKILLS

- Encourage ('I see ...;' 'I understand ...;' 'That's a good point.')
- Empathise/Identify ('I imagine that must have been very difficult for you.')
- Clarify ('Would you say that again? I'm not sure I fully understood.')
- Reflect back ('What I understand you are saying is . . .')

NON-VERBAL LISTENING SKILLS

- Sit at an angle, not square on (avoids confrontational feel);
- Keep an open stance (encourages openness in the speaker);
- Lean forward (shows interest);
- Make eye contact (avoiding eye contact suggests you've lost interest);
- Relax (a tense listener will cause the speaker to feel nervous). You may want to give examples of each point as you go along. None of these skills will guarantee good listening but they may help to set the tone for it.

> **HELPFUL HINT:**
>
> SOLER is a good way to help your group to remember non-verbal listening skills when they begin to connect with their community for real:
>
> **S**it
> **O**pen
> **L**ean
> **E**ye contact
> **R**elax

Barriers (5-10 mins)

Hope, Timmel and Hodzi identify the barriers to communication listed below.[3] Copy each onto separate pieces of card and hand them out, or alternatively read them out to the group as a whole. Then:

- Break down into groups of no more than five people.
- Give each group a set of title cards and a set of the descriptions.
- Ask them to match them together. If they were really listening to you earlier they will know immediately!

In and out listening	Most people think four times faster than they speak, so when listening there is a lot of spare thinking time, which can lead to you thinking about quite unrelated issues to what's being said. You can end up listening to only half of what is being said.
Red rag listening	Certain words or phrases may trigger an instantaneous emotional reaction in us – like showing a red rag to a bull. We take the word out of context and immediately stop listening.

| Closed mind listening | We can very quickly jump to conclusions about what is being said – 'I've heard this all before ...;' 'This is going to be boring ...;' 'I know more than they do' – and shut our minds to what is being said. This can also happen if we don't like or disagree with what is being said. |
| Over the head listening | What the person says is too complicated or confusing for the listener to understand, and just goes straight over the head. |

DISCUSSION POINTERS:

- On what occasions have you found yourself engaging (or not) in any of these types of listening?
- What are the reasons why you might have responded to what was being said in this way?
- What barriers do you find inhibit your listening?
- In what ways might you overcome some of these barriers? (For example, if the person finds the content of the conversation too complicated, ask them to clarify what they mean.)

PART B: OPEN QUESTIONS

When we talk to people we need to allow them to express their views – you already know your own! It is easy to fall into the trap of asking questions which allow for only one answer (leading), can only be answered with one word (closed), or which aren't questions, but statements of our views with a question mark tacked on the end. As the session moves on to practise questions that help to open people up to say more (open), it will consider the need for open questions and encourage the group to begin to develop questions that they could use for their community research. You may feel a simple game will provide a natural break from the listening exercises above.

Seek and you shall find (10-20 mins)

Hand out a sheet of questions based on your community research. Structuring your questions carefully will help you to recall some of the observations the group will have made during their walk in the community. If you have time you could develop it into a mini treasure hunt. Some questions might even require your group to ask questions of local people. Be careful though: 30 people asking one shopkeeper how much a quarter of bonbons costs could become annoying! Choose your 'question people' wisely and always get their permission. The game may highlight how easy it is to miss things even when we feel we are concentrating; however, its primary purpose is to provide experience of what it is like to get asked and to ask different styles of questions, e.g.:

● How would you describe the facilities at the local school?

● How do you feel when you walk down Swinburne Road?

● Do you agree that Birchgate Lane has six trees?

● How many shops are open on a Sunday in Highbury Close?

● At what time of night do you feel the noise coming from the Pig and Whistle becomes unacceptable?

Sorting the questions you developed for the exercise above into the relevant boxes on the grid below may help your group to recognise different styles of questioning. This should help to inform their thinking as they move on to activities designed to develop their own set of open questions.

	Factual	Experiential	Leading
Open	e.g. What is the area like for children?	e.g. How do you feel about living in this area?	e.g. I expect you will have a different view. Would you like to share it with us?
Closed	e.g. How many children live in the street?	e.g. When have you felt like giving up?	e.g. Don't you think such a view is irresponsible?

Practice makes perfect (20 mins)

At times asking a closed question is appropriate (such as when seeking clarification to make sure that you have understood what the person has said). However, especially in the early stages, open questions are crucial if you want to hear and understand people's real views.

● Divide your group into pairs.

● Ask each pair to develop a series of *open* questions that would help them to find out more about a person's views on their community, such as:
  – Who do you think are the most vulnerable people in our community?
  – What do you think are the main stresses of living in this community?
  – Where do most people go to relax?
  – When are people willing to help each other out?

● Each pair should then join another pair.

● One person from Pair A should ask one person from Pair B their questions. The other two people should observe both the effect of the questions and the listening style of the questioner.

● After two or three minutes, the group should *stop* and then
  – Give feedback on the questioners' listening style
  – Discuss how open each question was and whether they felt they provided enough scope for the other person to share their views
  – Decide what amendments to their questions and/or their listening style need to be made and repeat the role-play once more

● Repeat the process with one person from Pair B asking one person from Pair A their questions.

● To conclude, bring the small groups together again to feedback to the whole group any lessons they have learnt.

> **HELPFUL HINT:**
>
> Draw up a list of especially good questions from the groups' feedback. This list, with some adaptation, can be used when talking with the wider community.

Misleading others? (20 mins)

Read John 4:1-42 together.

First ask them, in groups of three, to answer the following questions. (The object of this exercise is to illustrate how superficially we tend to approach both our reading and our conversations with others.)

● How many times does the writer use a word beginning with 'w'?
Answer: almost 90 times.

● Out of the three top 'w's, which does he use the most? Water, woman or worship?
Answer: 'water' with 10, then 'woman' with nine, then 'worship' with six.

Make the point that this is often how we read the Bible and also how we read others – quickly, paying little attention to their needs, and missing the key points. You might like to use the following questions to understand the passage in more depth:

POINTS FOR REFLECTION

● Why do you think the disciples were so surprised to see him talking to the woman (v. 27)? Why was she so surprised (v. 9)?

The woman would have been marginalised for a number of reasons: she was a woman; she was a Samaritan; and some say she may have been a prostitute (though others doubt this and say she had just been married five times); either way, she was certainly living with someone who presumably wouldn't marry her.

BIBLICAL BACKGROUND

The Samaritans were held in contempt as religious rebels who had mixed the purity of Israel's worship with idolatry and the worship of pagan gods (cf. 2 Kgs. 17:24-41; Ezra 4:1-3; Sirach 50:25-26). The animosity toward the Samaritans was greatly intensified about 20 years before Jesus' ministry when some Samaritans defiled the temple in Jerusalem by scattering human bones in the courtyard during Passover (Josephus' *Antiquities of the Jews* 18.30). This conflict at the temple highlights one of the fundamental differences between the Samaritans and the Jews, namely the question of where God has centred his worship.[4]

Men could divorce women fairly easily but not vice versa. One possible reason for five husbands could have been her inability to produce children – which would also have made her feel like an outsider so that she had to come for water when no one else did.

● List some of the individuals or people groups who make up your community. In what ways are you quick to judge? What do you see first: potential or problems?

You have already thought about how people will make up their mind about you by reading your body language before you even open your mouth. Apparently we make up our mind about someone within the first 10 seconds of meeting them, either by what they wear, look like or smell.

● How does the woman's understanding of Jesus develop with the more time she spends with him? Make a list of the different assumptions she makes about who he is.

a thirsty man (v. 7), Jew (v. 9), a Rabbi or teacher (v. 11), Prophet (v. 16), Messiah (v. 29) and finally a Saviour (v. 42) – at least for others

● What would have happened if she had not stuck around to listen to him? Why did she?

In listening to the woman, Jesus sets an example for her to follow: she listens to him. Jesus saw the potential in a marginalised person, perhaps in ways we often don't. Jesus sets a good example of how to take an interest in someone and how to get them to open up. He appeals to her sympathy, curiosity, desire for ultimate satisfaction and, according to some, conscience (the 'go and call your husband' question). The key to good listening is to be really interested in the person we are speaking with: to love them, respect them and to want to bless them. This way you focus on them and getting to know them. In order to fully connect with people we need to capture some understanding of what Jesus feels for people – so *pray*!

SESSION 9

LISTEN: METHODS FOR EFFECTIVE COMMUNITY CONNECTION

Aim: To explain and practise a range of different skills that could be useful as the group begins to listen to the needs of their community.

You will need: Bibles, A4 paper, a selection of workshop electives (see pp. 99–109)

Questionnaires (30 mins)

Questionnaires are often the first thing that people think of when they think of finding out the needs of their community. Ask the group what experience they have had of using questionnaires before.

How did people respond?

● What worked well?

● What worked badly?

How do you respond to questionnaires?

● What has worked well?

● What has worked badly?

Ask the group what the possible advantages of questionnaires might be. *Answers might include: that they are quick, that every person is asked the same questions, that it is easier to process the results, that they are easier for group members to use than open-ended questions, and are able to reach more people, etc.*

Ask the group what the potential problems with questionnaires might be. Should you choose to use questionnaires as a way to connect with your community, you will need to decide on suitable solutions to the potential problems your group has identified. The following grid may help:

Potential Problem		Suitable Solution
feels officious	so	make it informal
feels like being put in a box	so	allow people to use their own words
space only for one-liners	so	be flexible
people too busy	so	keep it short
suspicion of strangers	so	put a card through the door a few days beforehand
misleading answers	so	use other tools to cross-check your findings
trying to find out too much	so	be clear on its purpose

A good way to test out a questionnaire and to provide practice is for people to try it out on each other first. Using some of the questions recorded in previous sessions, ask your group to write a draft questionnaire. Explain to the group what the questionnaire approach involves (e.g. knocking on doors, etc.).

AS A WHOLE GROUP (10 MINS)

Brainstorm the kind of reactions you might encounter from people (e.g. interest; disinterest; irritation).

IN SMALL GROUPS (10 MINS)

- Decide on a certain 'reaction' and role play a typical encounter on the doorstep.
- Discuss ways of dealing with this kind of situation.
- Rewrite a questionnaire that aims to avoid this problem.

IN PAIRS (10 MINS)

- Give one person a copy of a draft questionnaire and try it out.
- Discuss how the questions or questioner's style could be improved and feed back to the whole group.
- Allow the pairs to swap roles and try out the amended questionnaire again.
- Feed back any final points. By the end, you will have a questionnaire that has been tried and tested by the people who will be using it. If people still feel a bit nervous about it, encourage them to try it out on family and friends before going onto the streets. Here is an example:

COMMUNITY QUESTIONNAIRE

1. What do you like most about living in _____?

2. Is there anything you don't like about living here? Why?

3. What do you think are the most important issues in the community? Why?

4. Who are the people who need help in this community? Why?

5. If you could change one thing in this community what would it be? Why?

6. Would you be interested in knowing the result of this survey?

   If yes, please give your:

   Name:

   Address:

Selective electives (45 mins)

The next 40 minutes should be used to encourage members of your group to choose different workshops. Offer the following connection methods as taster workshops of about 20 minutes in length. They are designed to raise awareness of the different methods, and to develop new skills of connection. These will become useful during this second stage of the Express Community process. You may like to invite additional leaders to facilitate these groups; alternatively ask people from within the group to prepare an elective prior to the session. During the 40 minutes, group members should get the chance to choose two from the following:

- Community Mapping
- Chatting
- Interviewing
- Focus Groups
- Historical Profiling

EXPRESS TOGETHER

SUBJECTIVE CONNECTING

Choose to include any or all of the following connection methods, designed for use as 'tasters' as part of your *listen* session:

1. COMMUNITY MAPPING

YOU WILL NEED:

some blank paper (wallpaper lining if you decide to do it as one small group) and a pack of coloured pens.

Hand out a blank sheet of A4 paper to each person in your group, along with a pack of coloured pens or crayons. Read out the following instructions:

Draw it (15 mins)

ACTION	PEN COLOUR
Draw a map of your community/area/high street.	Black
Are there any areas where you don't feel safe?	Red
Where do young people 'hang out'?	Blue
Where do most people spend their leisure time?	Green
Where do most people work?	Grey
Where are the best places to live?	Pink
Where are the worst places to live?	Brown
Where do you like to spend most of your time?	Yellow
Mark what you would most like to see changed/improved/added.	Purple

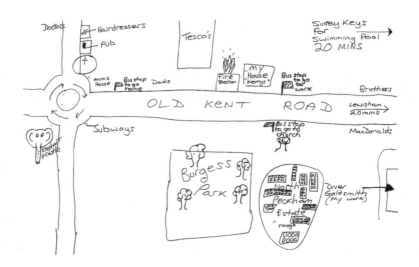

Discuss it (5 mins)

What the group do and don't draw can reveal a huge amount about its view of the community. The drawings can also serve as a great discussion starter on what members of the group think are local issues and needs.

EXPRESS EXPERIENCE

At a workshop where the cumulative total of people's experience of living in the community was more than 900 years, six different groups drew a map of their community, and then wandered around to see what the other groups had drawn. When they were asked what struck them most, they all pointed out the lack of services and amenities in the community (there were no shops, garages, or pubs within walking distance). Even though they had all lived in the community for so long, as car drivers they had never really thought about it before. Then the penny dropped as to the difficulties that elderly people or those without cars must have in their community, and that their building was one of the few facilities easily accessible. This led them to look on the potential for their building in a whole new light.

DISCUSSION POINTERS:

● What did you learn about your community?

● What did you learn about others' views of your community?

● How would you use this with the wider community? Who with (schools, young people on street corners, etc)?

● What questions might you want to pose at the end of the exercise?

2. CHATTING

YOU WILL NEED:

A4 paper that looks like a basic week-to-view diary (photocopy one from an old diary if you like), flip chart paper, pens, blank pieces of A6 card or paper, a watch or a timer, a bell or a buzzer to signify the end of each round

As well as not always being the most appropriate way of accessing valuable information, approaching people with questionnaires will fill some of your group with the feeling of dread. It may be helpful for them to consider a more informal approach. Chatting is a very good and non-threatening way of gathering information, and it is something that almost everyone can join in with, as it's a natural part of most people's everyday life. Encourage your small group to think more about chatting.

People (5 mins)

One of the best ways of beginning to identify the needs and issues in your community will be through chatting to people.

Hand out your week-to-view diary sheets and ask individuals to think about the different people they meet in a typical week. If this is difficult, get them to think about this with relation to the last week, which should be relatively fresh in their memory. Their entries might include meeting their mates, a barperson, the shopkeeper, the people with whom they work/study or their family members.

Discuss you entries in your small group (writing all the different people on flip chart paper for the whole group to see).

Points (5 mins)

Just as you talk with people about the weather, the football, the TV soap, the latest political scam, why not talk to them about the community? You probably already do. What do they think are the big issues facing the community? Get people talking and listen to what they say. We chat about a huge range of different subjects with no fear of freezing; no fear of our questions running dry; no fear of being made to look silly. Most of us are 'expert' chatters!

Hand out blank pieces of paper or card and in pairs ask each group to write down as many different one-word issues or subjects that you imagine might crop up whilst conversing with all these different types of people.

Practise (10 mins)

- Still in twos or threes, encourage them to practise chatting.
- Ask each group to pass their pile of issue/subject cards to the group on their left.
- Spend two or three minutes chatting about each issue.
- At the end of each 'round' a bell will ring to signify that you should move on to the next subject. Continue this simple exercise until you feel people have had enough. Emphasise that chatting should never feel forced and should be completely natural, but if it is to be effective people will need to know a little about the issues that concern their community.

EXPRESS EXPERIENCE

A group in Wales undertook a questionnaire survey of 4,000 homes in their local area. They became discouraged when after several weeks they had only covered 400 homes. Further questioning by the facilitator of the group revealed that the problem was that members kept being invited into people's homes to discuss things further over a cup of tea. They soon became encouraged when they were helped to realise that the informal information they had gathered through chats was worth more than any number of completed questionnaires.

3. INTERVIEWING

YOU WILL NEED:

A flip chart, BluTak, blank pieces of A6 card or paper, pens, two containers

Interviewing is one stage up from informal chatting. It is a tool for sitting down with key people in the community and tapping into some of their experience, knowledge and understanding of the issues through asking both prepared and spontaneous questions, with a flexible agenda that allows the interviewees freely to share their views.

Individuals (5 mins)

Interviews can use many of the same questions as a questionnaire, but a flexible agenda will help interviewees freely to share their views. Questions may also be far more specific and quite different depending on your interviewee. For example, the questions you ask your local butcher might differ from those that you will ask a headteacher.

Identify key individuals in the community that you might like to interview, write their names/roles down on separate pieces of card and stick them to a flip chart or wall.

Are there any that you have missed?

People with unique insights into the community might include the local GP, headteacher, shopkeeper, publican, social worker, policeman or even people who are seen as the 'moving spirits' of the community – those local people who get things done, whom others turn to in times of crisis, people who are seen as the 'heart' of the community.

Issues (5 mins)

It is worth interviewing individuals who have a key insight into a particular issue. Their extra expertise or experience may provide invaluable understanding to tap into. For example, a youth worker, teacher, parent, policeman and young person would all have a valuable and different insight into the issue of juvenile crime.

- Identify some of the key issues that these people might have knowledge about, write them down on separate pieces of card and stick them to a flip chart or wall.
- Divide your group into two sides.
- Ask each member of one side to pick an INDIVIDUAL card from the wall and each member of the other side to choose an ISSUE.
- Ask individuals from each side to find a partner from the other to form a pair.
- Ask each pair to read out their INDIVIDUAL followed by the ISSUE they have picked; hopefully there will be some unusual combinations.

Interview (10 mins)

Still in pairs, discuss what particular angle their INDIVIDUAL might bring to this ISSUE. Develop a few questions that would be appropriate to ask such an individual during an interview. If you have time, turn the questions into a quick role-play. Act them out in your small group or later when you return to the main group. Remember to observe and debrief the role-play to see what could be improved for the real thing.

Conclude the workshop with the following top 10 tips for interviews (you could produce it as a handout if you prefer):

Q   Questions should encourage explanation from the interviewee rather than a simple yes or no answer. Who? Why? What? Where? When? and How? questions help to generate a lot of discussion and information. Rephrase key questions; for example, rephrase 'What are the main dangers facing your children?' so that it reads 'What do you worry about most when it comes to your children?'

U   Use jargon-free language: talk naturally and clearly. It is easy to alienate or undermine people by using unnecessarily complicated language. Also, a misunderstood question is likely to be met with a misunderstood answer.

E   Explain clearly at the beginning why you want to ask the questions. Explain the process your group is undertaking, and how this interview fits into the process.

S   Silence is important. Learn when not to talk! If people are slow at talking, or reluctant to speak, don't jump in with another question (which is the temptation if you are a little nervous). Often people will share more if you give them space to answer.

T   Talk less and listen more. Sometimes people will drop vital clues in a throwaway comment, and you may want to follow that up instead of pursuing your own line of questioning. Your role is to listen, not to persuade or win them over to your way of thinking.

I   Invest in people. View the interview as the start of a longer-term relationship rather than a one-off hit-and-run. Take an interest in what is of interest to them. Be sensitive and respectful. The person has a valuable viewpoint, even if it is not one with which you agree.

O   Observe and reflect upon the responses you get from different groups of people. Do older people tend to give different answers from those of younger people? Do those living in more affluent housing see the issues differently from those in poorer housing? If you note any trends, jot them down before you get home: you may find out something quite significant.

N   Note down a few short, clear questions relating to the information you want to obtain. If the interviewee dries up, you won't. Write down what is being said, not your own interpretation. Later you will be able to interpret the information, but it is better not to mix the two. If interviewing by yourself, jot down key points during the interview and write up fuller notes immediately afterwards. It is very difficult trying to decipher notes you wrote three weeks ago! The key to good interviewing is preparation beforehand and accurate recording during (you might want to use a tape or mini-disc recorder – if so, get permission).

S   Say thank you to the interviewee for their time.

?   Finish with a question. Ask people whether they would like a copy of a report of your findings at the end of the process – if you are able to provide one! Do they mind you speaking to them again?

4. FOCUS GROUPS

Focus groups are a relatively specialised way of Connecting within Community. You might feel this way of connecting is unsuitable for your group. You may think your group is too small, too young or simply too inexperienced. You may choose to offer it as a taster workshop; in fact this may help you to decide whether it is suitable or not to use later as you begin to implement the different steps of research required for Stage Two: Connecting within Community.

Focus group discussions are a way of digging beneath the surface by bringing a group of people together to discuss their community. By giving people the opportunity to bounce ideas and opinions off each other, act as checks and balances on what others say, and give you and others in the group immediate feedback, focus group discussions can prove to be a dynamic complement to individual chats and interviews.

With whom? (5 mins)

You may decide to set up groups specifically to look at the issues you have identified. These may be made up of people interested in discussing these issues. Alternatively, you could ask to attend existing groups (such as a parent and toddler group). See 'People Worth Listening To', which can be found as part of the *Express Together* section of Chapter 4.

How to set up a focus group discussion (5 mins)

There are many different ways you could set up a focus group discussion. Discuss some ideas within your small groups. Here are just a few:

1. During your informal chats, interviews or questionnaires, you may have begun to identify people who are particularly interested in what you are doing. Tell them how much you appreciate their interest and invite them along to a discussion group.

PROBLEM	COMMENT	SOLUTIONS	YOU MIGHT SAY...
Domination		Always give everyone the opportunity to contribute to the discussion. Don't allow one person to dominate the discussion. If necessary, interrupt them if they won't stop talking. You can do this without being negative.	'Those of you who haven't said anything yet – is there anything you want to add?' 'John, what you've just said is very interesting. What do others think about what John has said?'
Silence	Don't be afraid of silences. Often silence can be a very creative time to help people think more deeply about the issues. Trying to fill the silence with another question can sometimes prevent the discussion going to a deeper level.	Ask clear and simple questions. Obviously some silences are a result of confusion and are not helpful. Try to ask short questions which everyone will understand.	
Jargon	Some people may use complicated specialist language or struggle to say clearly what they mean.	If you are unsure of what a person is trying to say, probably others in the group are too. Rather than allowing that person's comment to be lost, repeat back to them what you think they mean and see if that is correct.	'So what you're saying is... Have I understood that right?'
Emotion	Observe the emotional temperature of the discussion.	Reflect back to the group what you see. If someone says something controversial or with which you strongly disagree, resist the temptation to start arguing back. Often others will challenge a view that is clearly wrong in the group. If not, you may want to ask yourself whether it's your own view that needs to be challenged!	'I'm picking up that people feel really strongly about this issue. Is that right? What do others think?'
Direction	Trying to understand what is being said, plan the next question, pick up the signals of people's body language, check to see that everyone's involved, and keep a simple record of what is being said is tricky.	At regular points pause and summarise your understanding of the discussion so far. This helps to make sure that no one gets left behind and to clarify what the group has agreed. It is a helpful way of preventing the discussion going round in an endless circle.	

2. Invite neighbours or groups of people you know round to one of your sessions for a drink, a meal, a barbecue (whatever is most natural in your community) and get them talking.

3. Key individuals in the community may be able to set up a focus group for you. For example, a teacher may be able to invite you into the school to run a number of discussion groups with various classes; a social worker may be able to put you in touch with the local support group.

4. Contact local community groups, explain what you are doing and ask whether you can come and talk to the group and listen to their views.

5. If you are a member of a local group, ask if you can spend some time at the next meeting discussing things.

Be creative! You will find the effort of bringing a group of people together well worth while. Even the fact of bringing a group together begins to address a large problem in our communities – that of isolation and loneliness. An ideal focus group size is about six to eight people, though it can work with smaller and larger groups providing you provide opportunities to break down into smaller groups.

Important things to bear in mind (10 mins)

Facilitating group discussions is a very real skill. A good facilitator will help each individual in the group to draw upon all his or her experience and understanding of the issues and to share with others, so that the group is able to develop a more complete and deeper picture of their community. Discuss potential problems as a group. Use the following table to help you to come up with some solutions:

5. HISTORICAL PROFILING

Historical profiling is a relatively specialised way of connecting with community. You might feel this way of connecting is unsuitable for your group – you may think your group is too small, too young or simply too inexperienced. You may choose to offer it as a taster workshop; in fact this may help you to decide whether it is suitable or not to use later as you begin to implement the different steps of research required for Stage Two: Connecting within Community. If you do use it, set it up with church or family members before moving on to wider community groups, e.g. an over-60's group. This way you'll slowly develop your group's confidence in using this particular method.

Historical profiling is a helpful way of getting people to think about the present and future by reflecting on the past. By getting a person or group to plot the history of the community or of an issue, a natural forum is provided for discussing issues of importance to them in more depth. A particularly appropriate group to do profiling with is the elderly. Often this may generate an initially rose-tinted view of the past. However, the things they identify as not being as good as they once were are obviously significant to them and worth exploring. Also an old person's sepia view of the past is often the equivalent of a younger person's vision of the future; it certainly gives a clear indication of their values and what matters to them – an invaluable thing to know in trying to understand the community, even if the factual content is somewhat misleading.

In a group setting it is positive to challenge some of the views, asking the group as a whole whether things really were this good/bad. Ask them to identify definite trends and the reasons for these. For example, tracing the drug culture on an estate over the last 15 years may reveal a rise in the use of certain drugs and a fall in the use of other drugs. It would be worth exploring the reasons for this.

Here is how to do it.

Decide (5 mins)

Decide on the theme of the historical profile. It could be as general as the history of the local community in the person's lifetime or as specific as changes to educational provision for truants in the last five years.

Draw (10 mins)

- Ask the person or group to draw a straight horizontal line across the page.
- Ask them to put the start date of their profile at the far left-hand side of the line.
- Then ask them to think about key events during the period and to mark them on their line in chronological order, putting those they see as positive events above the line, and events they see as negative below the line. Some people find it easier to do this going back from the present day; others find it easier starting from the earliest date and working forwards. Allow people the freedom to do it whichever way is easier for them.

Historical profile of an estate

Drawn by old age pensioners

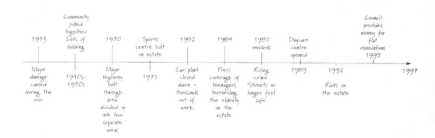

Discuss (5 mins)

Once they have completed the time-line, ask questions about it:

- Ask about the significance of the events they have listed.
- Ask the reasons for ranking an event positive or negative.
- Ask what lessons from the past they think it would be good to learn from.
- Ask what mistakes were made in the past that it is important to avoid.
- Ask the participants if they could continue drawing the time-line into the future what they would want to see happening and what they would be afraid of happening.

EXPRESS EXPERIENCE

A group in a Welsh mining community used the historical profiling tool. The three different groups all started off their time-line, quite independently of each other, with an event called the 'Gas Tank Wars' in the mid-1970s. This was an episode when the gas board decided to build two large gas tanks in the middle of the community. Everyone was up in arms about this, so every time the gas board van was seen driving into the village, someone would run down to the fire station and ring the bell. By the time the van reached the site, several hundred residents just standing there on the site would confront them. After a while the gas board got fed up and sited the tanks outside of the village. Everyone in the group spoke about this event with lots of pride and enthusiasm. When asked why, they replied it was because the community had come together and achieved something. The group facilitator's next question helped to galvanise the group to think about action: 'What issue today would bring the community together in fighting for a common cause?' For members of the group who were cynical about being able to change anything, the 'Gas Tank Wars' served as a useful reminder that things could indeed change.

---

[1] Derek Kidner, *Ezra and Nehemiah* (Leicester: IVP, 1979), p. 82.

[2] Cited in T. Raistrick, *Church, Community and Change: The Manual (Phase 2)* (Teddington: Tearfund, 2000), p. 10.

[3] T. Raistrick, *Church, Community and Change: The Manual (Phase 2)* (Teddington: Tearfund, 2000), p. 21. These barriers to communication have been adapted from A. Hope, S, Timmel and C. Hodzi, *Training for Transformation* (Zimbabwe: Mambo Press, 1984).

[4] I. H. Marshall, A. R. Millard, J. I. Packer and D. J. Wiseman, *New Bible Dictionary* (Leicester: IVP, 1996).

Some men came, bringing to him a **paralytic**, carried by four of them. Since they could not get him to Jesus because of the crowd, they made an **opening in the roof** above Jesus and, after digging through it, lowered the mat the paralysed man was lying on. When Jesus saw their faith, he said to the paralytic, 'Son, your **sins are forgiven**' (Mk. 2:3-5).

Chapter 4

THE VALUE OF INVOLVEMENT

'Why don't you turn off your TV and do something less boring instead?'[1] Or at least that was something like the question posed to a whole generation of kids by a programme of the same name during almost every summer break throughout the 1980's. Did they take any notice? Not a bit! The irony was that thousands of them across the country, after the initial shock of the opening credits, would have slumped back into their chairs and done absolutely nothing! So what will you do: seek out solutions within your community or slump and second guess? As you think through this second chapter of Stage Two: Connecting with Community, it is time to decide whether you are going to choose to involve others and turn on the theories of connecting – the methods, skills and principles you practised in Chapter 3 – or focus on your own agenda and do something less valuable instead. As you do so, you may find it helpful to consider the following key questions:

- Who in your community do you want to connect with?
- What do you hope to achieve as a result of Connecting within Community? What might get in the way of that?
- Why do you want to connect with your community? What is your motive?
- How will you, as leader, encourage your group and the community to see the value of Connecting within Community?

Perhaps you might be wondering whether you should be working with your community in identifying areas of need at all. Perhaps you feel you should do the work on their behalf. These are important questions, and your answers will set the tone for the way you and your group choose to continue in the Express Community process and ultimately what you decide to do as a result. As you consider the value of involvement, picture the feeling of kneeling side by side with a group of friends as together you tear up the barriers which for years have prevented you and your community from discovering Jesus' purpose for your lives. As you do so, you see the face of Jesus, quite literally who he is in the flesh. But what is he doing? He is welcoming you with open arms. Why? Because he wants to involve you in a process of change that will restore your life to the image he had in mind when he first created you. Imagine that!

INVOLVEMENT, A MODEL FROM JESUS

The healing ministry of Jesus provides some helpful lessons for your own involvement in the community. Jesus almost always healed in response to people: he expected people to participate, to get involved. Jesus showed his compassion not just by doing things *for* people, but by working *with* people as well.

Before we go any further, try and list as many of Jesus' healings as you can remember. The total number of healings is much larger, but the number of passages that refer to healings in the gospels is more than 30. All were chosen by the writers to illustrate important themes, and there is much we can learn from them today about Jesus' compassion, stirring him to action, and his desire to intervene in people's lives.

The purpose of this chapter, however, is to look at the way Jesus involved other people in the healings he performed.

Healing was a key part of Jesus' ministry. Jesus did perform other miracles, but healings were by far the most common. On the vast majority of these occasions, either the person in need or others in relationship with them were directly involved in either initiating or being part of the healing process. Jesus rarely initiated healing people, but rather waited for people to approach him – and he often involved people in bringing about their healing.

There are just six exceptions to be found in the four gospels. On three occasions Jesus initiated healing on the Sabbath, a day when through custom and religious regulations no one would have approached a holy man for healing: the healing of the man possessed by an evil spirit in the synagogue (Mk. 1:21-28; Lk. 4:31-37); the healing of a man with a shrivelled hand (Mk. 3:1-6; Mt. 12:9-14; Lk. 6:6-11); and the healing of a woman who had been crippled for 18 years (Lk. 13:10-17). People would not come to Jesus for healing on the Sabbath and so on these rare occasions Jesus came to them.

The other three exceptions are also unusual. Jesus heals the man possessed of an evil spirit in the region of the Gerasenes (Mt. 8:28-34; Mk. 5:1-20; Lk. 8:26-39). The man had been cut off from society: no one was in a position to ask for his healing and he himself was not in a fit state of mind to ask for healing himself. Jesus raised the son of a widow in Nain from the dead without being asked, an action so extraordinary it went beyond people's capacity to ask for it. And finally, Jesus healed the ear of the soldier attacked by a disciple in the Garden of Gethsemane, an act to demonstrate swiftly and powerfully that he had no intention of leading an armed rebellion.

On all the other 20 or more occasions recorded in the gospels where Jesus healed people, the sufferer or their friends and relatives were involved in some way. Jesus did not heal passive recipients: he expected people to participate, to get involved. He did things with people, not simply for them. On every occasion (apart from the exceptions noted above) Jesus healed in response to people. He didn't just jump in when he perceived a need and impose a solution, no matter how much it was needed. He waited, he listened, he allowed them to raise their concerns. Jesus showed his immense love and compassion for people by allowing them (or their friends and relatives) to initiate or get involved in the healing process – to step out in faith and work with him rather than just receive from him. To Jesus that seemed to be an important part of the healing process.

INVOLVEMENT, A MODEL FOR ALL

Having taken a quick glimpse at Jesus' method of involving others, it is time to consider how we might begin to interpret his model of integral mission in the way we choose to involve others in the gradual steps which build up to form Stage Two: Connecting within Community. For many people in our communities the barrier that exists between their needs and any notion that a Christian community may have about discovering their needs remains relatively untouched. In some areas in our communities the lid containing all their problems has been firmly in place for years.

Many communities, Christian and otherwise, may feel a long way from being in a position to see Jesus clearly enough even to begin to imagine what it might feel like to rest in his loving arms. Whether through a lack of concern, a lack of cause or a lack of commitment, nobody has shown them either the interest or inclination to suggest working together to overcome those things that are preventing them seeing Jesus and exposing his love. From where you are standing, it may seem that taking steps to open the way between you and your community seems a long way off.

As for reaching the feet of Jesus, even if you were to begin or you have begun, that feels like an awfully long way down. We often focus on the great lengths the paralysed man's friends went to get him onto the roof, but however difficult that may have been to get him there, their job was only half complete. Reaching the feet of Jesus was the aim: after all this is where the miracle would take place. Once on the roof the friends would have to negotiate the difficult task of finding a safe way for their friend to meet with Jesus.

Rather than allowing yourself to be daunted by the enormity of it all, or even paralysed by a fear of what lies ahead, now is the time to start caring. It is time to build on what you have learnt already and take some action. Are you feeling fearful? It may help at this point to read the words of Paul in Ephesians 3:14-21 as a prayer:

> *I pray that out of his glorious riches he may strengthen you with power through the Spirit in your inner being, so that Christ may dwell in your hearts through faith. And I pray that you, being rooted and established in love, may have power, together with all the saints, to grasp how wide and long and high and deep is the love of Christ, and to know this love that surpasses knowledge – that you may be filled to the measure of all the fullness of God. Now to him who is able to do immeasurably more than all we ask or imagine, according to this power that is at work in us, to him be the glory in the church and in Christ Jesus throughout all generations, for ever and ever! Amen.*

If no one decides to take hold of the potential to do something within your community then you could find yourself waiting for something to happen for years to come. So what can we do? How can we get involved and ensure others feel they can too?

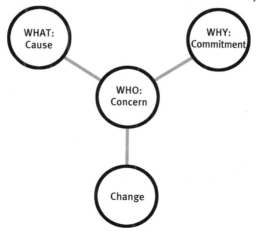

A CONCERN FOR INVOLVEMENT

As you begin to trample down some of the increasingly overgrown paths towards more remote parts of your wider community, you may find areas that you once considered greener than your own are littered with more problems than you imagined. Or it may be that you are surprised to find signs of life in what you thought were quite barren areas. Whatever you see, time and time again you'll find yourself hit by the harsh reality of people's frustration, resistance and woundedness from damaging experiences of people imposing change upon them and their lives. As you begin connecting within community take time to read the signs you come across. Do not allow your own assumptions to dictate whether you choose to offer some kind of fleeting recognition or stop to read between the lines. Look, stop and listen and you may be surprised at what you find. Maybe if you are prepared to slow down and take a more considered look you'll discover more about what really concerns your community. It may be phone masts, fox hunting or a concern about proposed flight paths. It could just as easily be loneliness, fear or a feeling of being ignored or neglected. When people feel strong enough about something, they are not afraid to speak up. The problem for many is that when they do speak up they don't always feel as though they are being heard.

LEARNING FROM LIFE

'No one asks our views. We see many millions of pounds wasted in inappropriate initiatives based on the very expensive advice of academic experts who have never lived in poverty. But we are the real experts of our own hopes and aspirations. Service providers should ask the users before deciding on policies, before setting targets that will affect our lives. We can contribute if you are prepared to give up a little power to allow us to participate as partners in our own future, and in the future of the country.'

Moraene Roberts, unemployed and registered disabled, speaking to church and political leaders at the National Poverty Hearing (March 1996).

Providing you are prepared to look closely enough, you will soon begin to see the depth of people's concerns. So far their concerns may have only been expressed in the stroke of a brush or pen, but maybe, as together you begin to explore the issues, they may see some potential for powerful change. The question is are you, are your group, prepared to listen? Can you even hear what people are saying above all the other things in your life that are constantly vying for your attention?

With all this potential information and increasing involvement, there is a danger that the Connecting within Community stage of *Express Community* could all become very confusing. The steps we are suggesting are designed to bring clarity to the process. However if you feel they are beginning to hinder you in your attempt to hear people's needs, then you may need to take some time to consider whether you need to adjust your stride. Your main aim is to connect with people and their very real needs; if you don't think you are dedicating enough energy to doing this, then maybe you need to slow down and take on less in order to give more. Make sure you encourage and empower people to make their own plans rather than impose your own detailed map of where you think you ought to go. Before you even consider sharing your own thoughts on what direction your concerns for neighbourhood might take you, be careful that in your haste to arrive at solutions you also allow yourself time to pull over and pause to give thought to other people's concerns. Take a break; it won't kill you!

A CAUSE FOR INVOLVEMENT

The more time you take to connect with corners of your community, the more you will probably come to ponder the cause of their protest. There are many reasons why people may feel so passionately that they choose to pledge allegiance to a cause. Does their involvement in occasional causes rise out of a realistic hope that their resistance will bring about positive results? Or is it more like a desperate last-ditch act of defiance? Whichever it is, you have to admire people's commitment to act on their concerns. What desperation does serve to illustrate is that despite what current cultural thinking may have us believe, people do sometimes care enough about some issues to move beyond themselves for the sake of other people, places or purposes.

On occasions when passions do run high, given the right cause, whether it is to save jobs, to search for a missing child, or to support an elderly member of the neighbourhood who has been robbed, some people are prepared to make a committed effort to widen their view of what community means for them. This should encourage you. Being prepared to come together to fight for the right cause demonstrates people's willingness to widen their ideas about their own corporate identity. The very fact that you have chosen to go through this Express Community process also shows that you too have decided to take steps to change your own ideas about your identity, particularly how you as a group relate to your community. As you seek to discover which 'worthy' cause to invest in as part of your integral mission, any sense of dissatisfaction with the current state of play is a connection you ought to look out for. Connecting with Community is about finding ways to get involved with your community that channel its initial concern for a cause.

A COMMITMENT TO INVOLVEMENT

Unfortunately, whatever the cause for a community united is, its formation is often made up of a relatively small squad of people, committed to a short-term game, played on a small-scale pitch. However passionate people may be at the start, with such a focused cause of concern the real value of their involvement tends to be limited. Though some teams do reach their goal, others go way off the mark or even fail to go the distance. After the roar of the kick-off, the crowd go silent, enthusiasm dies away, and as the memory of who, what, why and how it all began departs from people's minds, so do they. They take their eye off the ball and either get sent off in frustration, leave the field of play of their own accord or begin to look for someone to substitute them in their role. It is true that some corporate disappointment, disaster or dodgy decisions do leave a scar; their impact can make a neighbourhood richer or poorer, for better and worse.

EXPRESS EXPERIENCE

In a previous role as a community youth worker, I met people who would often recall how one local Christian man had been prepared to stand against plans to turn a local beauty spot into an open cast mine. Even though he had passed away some years before I took up my post people still remembered him, his connection with their lives and the fact that he was a Christian. His passion had caused others to stand with him and the beauty spot remains as a constant reminder of this.

If as Christians we could prolong the passion that under certain conditions rises from the heart of our community, then maybe we would begin to see signs of God's kingdom moving into our neighbourhood rather than the crude cardboard cutouts that can be seen all too often just going through the motions. The key to unlocking the potential for change within our communities is to identify the issue that will keep theirs, yours and your group's attention, and one which together you will be committed to seeing through. Only then can their initial concerns move beyond short-term commitment to discover what it means to bring about lasting positive change. Then they will feel it is something worth getting involved in. It is sad that it often takes disasters, personal tragedy or even minor inconvenience to convince people that working together to meet their needs is the most effective way to live together within community. Short-term or long term, wouldn't it be incredible if as part of the Express Community process people found ways simply to get on for good?

A CHANGE THROUGH INVOLVEMENT

The extent to which people feel they will want to commit to a cause will in many ways be determined by your role as leader in the whole process. In a kind of ripple effect, the way you demonstrate the value of involvement in your style of leadership – the good, the bad and the ugly bits – will naturally determine how your group in turn chooses to value the involvement of others. Anyone who has ever been led by an autocratic leader will know exactly how it feels to be pushed into something you really don't want to do. To be led by someone who is controlling and only allows his or her own ideas to be implemented can be incredibly demoralising, constrictive and oppressive. Maybe you're sure you are not like that. But if you're honest, sometimes it's hard not to be, particularly when you have so much to do and what seems so little time to do it in. Occasionally, among friends, family or colleagues, you may drift into autocratic mode. Occasionally it's excusable, but when it comes to leading your group and then in turn them leading your community through the Express Community process, it is most definitely not on. Despite what you think, your ideas about bringing life to an integral mission within your community can wait. Take your time; this is not a race! If you push ahead in a rush, you could end up hurting people rather than honouring their involvement. Pushing people because of a pressure to perform is pointless.

'Ownership', feeling a part of something, greatly affects people's attitude. Without ownership, people very easily become disinterested and disillusioned and may even try to sabotage a project. As leader, are you going to take suggestions on board? Are you going to listen?

LEARNING FROM LIFE

At a leadership training session in the South of England the facilitator divided the participants into two groups, allocating each a leader, and handing out a number of shapes cut from five 18cm x 18cm pieces of card (similar to the ones below).

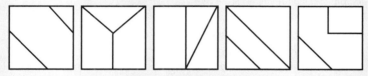

Each leader was given the task of explaining to their group that all the shapes made five equal-sided squares. Their task was to make up those squares. What the groups were not told was that one leader had been briefed to play the role of an autocratic, controlling leader, who would take suggestions on board providing they were said in a suitably humble way, although they might claim them as their own. In contrast the other leader had been asked to be much more consultative and democratic, asking people for their opinion, valuing their contributions, and seeking to draw all members of the group into participation. They were there to facilitate the group in coming up with a solution, not to impose their answer on the group. The results were surprising! The people in the autocratic leader's group got fed up with how the leader was behaving and started sabotaging the activity, hiding pieces of the squares, deliberately ignoring instructions, or just removing themselves from the entire process. In the 'listening' leader's group, by contrast, people were laughing and fully engrossed in the task; they even cheered when they finished! Even though people knew it was a game, they quickly became influenced by how they were being treated – a powerful lesson.

Perhaps you are more consultative and democratic than autocratic. You do ask for people's opinions, value their contributions, and seek to draw people into participating. You are prepared to facilitate for people as they come up with their own solutions. If this is you, great! Ensure you remain that way! With ownership, people pull together, share the burden and achieve the aim in a much more positive atmosphere. Whether or not your group choose to listen to their community and are prepared to go that extra mile in involving others in what they do will largely be determined by you and what you model to them.

HELPFUL HINT:

Try the shape exercise with your group. See how they respond to being involved or not involved in the decision-making process – it may help to inform their thinking as they begin to consider the attitude in which they should approach this stage of Connecting within Community.

Just like your group, your community's desire to get involved will be determined by whether or not they feel they have a role to play and whether they feel what they have to say is worth saying, is worth listening to and will actually be acted upon. The best way to start to open your community's eyes to a whole range of choices for change is to get them involved in that process from the start. This participative approach leads to better quality decisions, which can then be more effectively implemented. Huczynski and Buchanan (2004), discussing the value of this in leadership and management, state that:

> *A participative style can improve organisational effectiveness by tapping the ideas of people with knowledge and experience, and by involving them in decision-making processes to which they then become committed. People who are involved in setting standards or establishing methods are thus more likely to:*

> - *accept the legitimacy of decisions reached with their help*
> - *accept change based on those decisions*
> - *trust managers who actually make and implement decisions*
> - *volunteer new and creative ideas and solutions*[1]

Why wait until you think you have the solution before involving people in the Express Community process? Why not encourage others to be involved as you seek to find the causes for the potential problems they raise. Show them that they have a part in the process, that they are significant and integral to what goes on in your community – as are you and your group. In order to be committed to change, people need to see they have a role, are given responsibility and will be respected for what they are considering contributing. This will be key as your group begins to connect with the people they meet in their community.

TOWARDS A CONCLUSION THROUGH INVOLVEMENT

As we approach some sort of conclusion to this brief exploration of involvement, we return to the questions posed at the outset of the chapter:

- Should you be working with your community in identifying areas of need at all?
- Should you do the work on their behalf?

How you decide to answer these questions personally, and how you as a group choose to offer *Express Community* as one way of finding a cause will determine how passionate everybody will be about contributing ideas and staying involved. A key part to identifying real needs is to involve the people who have them. Not only does it mean we are able to get to the heart of the problem but it gives them the confidence to believe that their experience and ideas are valuable and worth listening to. We all appreciate being allowed to make a contribution and get involved in something worthwhile, which gives us worth. We all like being offered the opportunity to take part in something, especially if it affects us. And surely a process that offers change for the better is preferable to a feeling of going nowhere in the hope that things won't change for the worse?

Then, when we have heard from people, we need to work with them, not simply for them. The way Jesus chose to involve people in every aspect of his integral mission, from the minor to the miraculous, provides a clear model for us to follow as we seek to express community. Of course the very nature of Jesus' lifestyle and the very openness of his character meant that people were willing to come to him because they knew he was willing to serve. Unfortunately Christians often have a much less positive track record. People don't see the Christian community as a natural place to voice their concerns or seek healing, of whatever kind. As Christians, before we can begin responding to a community in need, we need to become more proactive and disciplined in the way we choose to get people involved in the process of listening, going and finding out what their real needs are. What will it say about you, if as a group you make a concerted effort to connect with those whom society spends most of its time ignoring: the poor, the elderly, the alienated, and those in need. Not only is it more effective in the long term, it values people in a way that imposing 'help' on people can never do. Listening is an important act of serving our community in itself. It could be that one of the people's needs in your community is that of simply needing someone to listen to them. Even at this stage you could be beginning to express community.

KEY QUESTIONS

As you consider whether or not to involve people in this stage of the Express Community process, it may help to think of occasions when you have been unfortunate enough to be on the other end of an autocratic leader. The exercise outlined below might help; try it with your group or a team of leaders if you have them. Ask yourself:

1. *Whose* style of leadership most inspires you? Why? What are the positive and negative aspects of their style? How are you left feeling as a result of being included in making decisions?

2. *What* type of leader would you say best describes you? If a leader took a similar approach with you, how willing would you be to be a part of their group? How might this impact the way you express community in your personal life, in your group and in the community itself?

3. *Why* do you think you lead the way you do? In what ways do you feel it is effective? How do you think it makes people feel? How might a similar model make your community feel about *Express Community*? What would Jesus challenge, change or compliment about the way you value involvement?

4. *How* do you feel when a task is not fully explained to you? Do you want to get involved? Why? Why not?

From experience of various types of leadership, do your feelings and attitudes towards a task change as time goes on? Why? Have you always finished what you started? If you do, how do you feel when you finish something? Are you satisfied or do you lose interest? If you don't tend to complete what you have started, how do you feel when you don't?

ENGAGE YOUR GROUP
EASY-TO-USE SESSION PLANS

HOW TO STRUCTURE THE CONNECTING WITHIN COMMUNITY STAGE

The earlier you and your group decide how to structure the Connecting within Community stage, the better. Identifying the needs of your community can appear to be a massive task. Once you start, it may appear even bigger! It is recommended that you take the following approach to keep the information gained from your listening both useful and manageable. However you may feel you need to do less. Ask yourself, 'What has already been done?' 'What is feasible?' You should at least consider doing steps one and two, or two and three. The sessions may appear quite structured, but remember they are a guide to use in a way that best fits with your group and your community. It is important for your group to get into the habit of listening to and learning from the community. The connecting methods they practised in previous chapters will help them to do this.

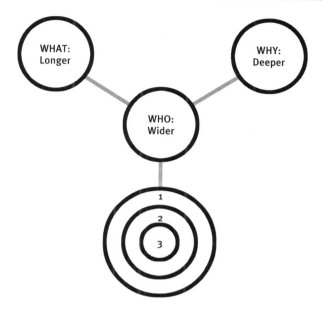

Step 1: Look wider

Research: Ask as many people as possible what they see as the major needs and issues in their communities. If you do not do this, you may not pick up on what people see as the big issues and instead you may end up with a 'wish list' of 101 things.

Review: As a group, review the findings and focus on four to six key issues or themes. (Session 11 is designed to help you with this.)

Step 2: Stop and go longer

Identify: Which people, both within and outside the church, have insights into these key issues?

Ask: Why is the issue important? What causes this issue? What impact does it have?

Review: Come back together and share your findings. Discuss what you have found out and try to identify what you see to be the crux of the issues. (Session 12 will help you with this review.)

Step 3: Listen deeper

Check: Go back to some of the people you have talked to and possibly some outside 'experts' on those particular issues and ask them what they think about your findings.

- Do these conclusions seem right?
- Do they have any ideas for ways to respond to the issues identified?

Review: Prioritise the needs and plan the way ahead. Invite everyone who has been involved to the Acting within Community workshops to share your findings and conclusions, and together work on how to respond in a practical way. (See the Acting within Community sessions in Chapter 5.)

AIMING HIGHER (EPHESIANS 3:18-19)

Reasons for this approach

Groups often encounter problems if after starting broad they never focus. They end up with a 'wish-list' of 101 needs they would like to address, with which they can do little. Other groups sometimes experience the opposite problem. They start off having already made up their minds about what the problem is, and check out their conclusions with a few people in the community just to show they have consulted with people! The consultation is inadequate and can lead to inappropriate decisions being made.

The Connection within Community process at a glance

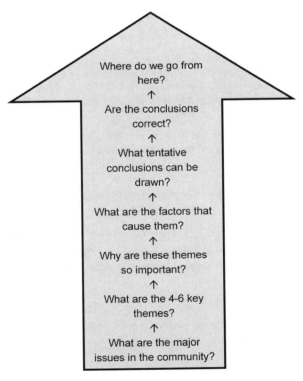

Where do we go from here?
↑
Are the conclusions correct?
↑
What tentative conclusions can be drawn?
↑
What are the factors that cause them?
↑
Why are these themes so important?
↑
What are the 4-6 key themes?
↑
What are the major issues in the community?

START

SESSION 10

LOOK WIDER

Step 1 of Connecting within Community

Aim: To recognise and build upon how people in the group are already involved in the community. To plan where and how you should begin to listen to your community.

YOU WILL NEED:

Bibles, completed or new Community Mapping sheets (from Session 1, Chapter 1), Information Summary sheets (see Express Together at the end of this chapter – an A4 version is available online at www.expresscommunity.org). You will also need help from a couple of others in the group in writing down feedback on large sheets of paper after each activity.

Common People (10 mins)

As your group enter the session, hand each person a copy of the grid below and ask them to find different people in the room who can say 'yes' to what is in each box. When they find someone, they should write their name in the box. Continue until one person has completed a line or the whole grid.[3]

wears glasses	plays an instrument	owns a car	has black hair	enjoys reading	still has tonsils
eats meat	sings in the shower	is a bad swimmer	can curl their tongue	has long nails	likes roller-coasters
is wearing blue socks	can do a hand-stand	has broken an arm	hates milk	loves cabbage	has flown in a plane
enjoys long journeys	owns a road map	watches daytime TV	has used the Tube	enjoys studying	has done a parachute jump

The key to the first stage of connecting with your community is to ask, and listen, to as many people as possible. This way you'll be able to get an insight into the major needs and issues which exist within your community. Previous sessions have discussed the skills required for effective connection, but this session is primarily designed to get you started. It will focus on:

1. Who needs to be listened to

2. What skills you will require

3. Who will listen to whom and when

● ●

Who to listen to (20 mins)

In Step One, you want to network with as wide a cross-section of people as possible. Later in Steps Two and Three, you can begin to focus down more specifically, having identified your key areas.

Ask you group to make a list of the key people to speak to and listen to.

The list of 'People worth listening to', which forms part of Express Together at the end of this chapter (pp. 135-136), might help you to think about the kind of people you need to be listening to in your community. It is not designed to be comprehensive, but will help you get started. The 'gate-keepers' (those with particular insights into the community) have been listed under different sub-sections, but many of them will give valuable insights into more than just that one theme.

Of course, the person you need to listen to most is God. Praying here may help you to think about people you have missed and those who deserve special attention. It will also help to inform the decisions you will make.

● ●

Who's listening to whom? (20 mins)

Once you have a list of people in the community who need to be heard, the next step is to link these names with people in the group who would be able to talk and listen to them. A good way to decide who should talk to whom is to either:

a) Allocate people to specific people groups, issues or places according to where they may have already walked during Session 7: 'Look' (Chapter 3),

or

b) Use the map of the activities your group produced during Session 1: 'Belonging to community' (Chapter 1) to highlight any links they may already have with groups and individuals in the community.

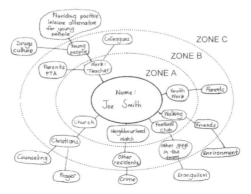

Having raised your own level of confidence and understanding of the issues, you will want to start talking to people you do not know. This is important! If you restrict yourself to the people you know, you will encounter the same, or at any rate similar, backgrounds, cultures and perspectives on the issues. Try the following approach:

- Involve as many people in your group as possible.
- Start listening inside your group/wider church community.
- Listen to friends, neighbours and others.
- Listen to community groups, such as the scout group, the parent and toddler group, or the dog training club.
- Listen to others outside the church, such as councillors, the regeneration officer, or members of the youth offenders team.

Choosing your methods (20 mins)

As well as deciding who in your group will talk and listen to whom, you will need to decide how they will do this. What methods will you use? Recap on the different methods available and when they are most suitably used:

METHOD	BEST USED WITH	FOUND ON p.
1. *Questionnaires* (forms useful to gather a large amount of information quickly)	individuals you don't know	96
2. *Community mapping* (drawing a map of the local area)	individuals; groups	100
3. *Chatting* (when an informal approach is best)	individuals; informal groups	101
4. *Interviewing* (for asking questions in a more formal setting)	key individuals in the community	103
5. *Focus group discussions* (for getting a group to discuss issues)	groups	105
6. *Historical profiling* (drawing a time-line)	individuals; groups	107
7. *The goldfish bowl* (Technique for helping people to listen to each other)	groups	128

| 8. *But why? flow charts* (asking 'But why?' to dig beneath the surface) | individuals; groups | 131 |

When (20 mins)

The final decision you will have to make at Step One is a suitable time to carry out the research. Connecting, whether through talking or listening, does not happen by accident and so it will be necessary to plan. The process may seem long-winded but planning in the details helps.

Planning provides *roles*, which ensures everyone in the group is involved; you should be able to find methods that match the different skills and level of confidence of each of your group members.

Planning produces *records*, which should demonstrate a clear picture of what research is happening, who is doing it and with whom. Clear records will make your job of supporting, encouraging and occasionally chasing up group members much easier.

Planning provides a *reminder* to let people know when, where and what they need to do. It should also help to prevent unnecessary overlap, i.e. Mrs Smith being asked about her problem with 'X' by four different people on six different occasions.

Planning produces *results*, not simply at the end, but at every stage of the process. Your planning should lead to a continual process of discovery. As issues or places have been researched it is important to keep people updated on the results by clearly communicating your progress. Good planning is the ideal way to build a step-by-step sense of achievement.

You could use the following pro forma to record all the relevant information:

People group, issue or place	Who? (person/s responsible for contacting them)	When? (deadline by which this should happen)	Why? (specific information you might like to find out)	Skill? (appropriate skill for this individual/ group)	Completed (when it was achieved)

SESSION 11

STOP AND GO LONGER

Step 2 of Connecting within Community

Aim: To provide a simple format to review the findings of Step One of the connecting process and to prepare the group for Step Two – identifying specific issues or needs.

YOU WILL NEED:

a Bible, water pistol, paper, Post-It notes (optional), pens, Information Summary sheets

Preparation:

Prior to the session it will be important to collate and sort all the feedback. As leader you might like to take responsibility for this task at the end of Step One.

- Count how many people are represented.
- Note the age, gender and geographical spread. Are there areas of the community or age groups that are under-represented?
- Identify the common answers. Are there any differences in the kind of answers given by people of different generations or different parts of the community?
- Compare this information with some of the more formal statistics you may have got from census forms and local government surveys (refer back the results of your 'Objective Connecting' carried out as part of Express Together at the end of Chapter 1). Are there common issues and general trends emerging? After this session, should you decide that forming individual issue groups is the best way to continue the Connection process, then collating research will become the responsibility of each individual group.

Making the connections (15 mins)

You will need a water pistol and maybe some towels for this activity!

- Arrange the group in a circle.
- Standing in the centre, call out a key word or phrase from the research which you have collated prior to the meeting, such as 'loneliness', 'drugs', 'litter', etc.
- Think of another word that relates to the word you have chosen.
- Speak out that word.
- In turn ask each member of the group to do the same. If they repeat your/another player's word or hesitate – eliminate them from the game by squirting them.

Careless whispers? (10 mins)

As you begin to consider the needs of your community, reflect for a minute on what issues God might be calling you towards. Read 1 Kings 19:9-13, where the LORD appears to Elijah, not in a powerful wind, an earthquake, a fire, or even a jet of water, but in a gentle whisper. As your group splits into smaller groups to consider some of the results of their research, stress the importance of not missing key issues simply because they are not the ones shouting the loudest. Decisions about which areas deserve your attention should not be left to a purely logically cerebral exercise: you will require God's wisdom.

Spend some time praying, reflecting or meditating before moving on to the next stage of the session.

●●●

The goldfish bowl (30 mins)

This connection method will help group members to reflect upon their own experience of the community and to listen to the experiences of other people. Half of the group reflects on their experience of the community or a specific issue, while the rest of the group listens and observes. It is recommended for use within your own group, however if you know of other groups who would respond well, you could use it with them as well. *Try to keep it as simple as possible to avoid confusion. It can be very difficult to manage with more than 12-15 in the group.* As people listen and then reflect on what they hear, the level of discussion can be much more thoughtful.

1. Divide your group into two and ask one group (A) to form a circle in the centre of the room. The other group (B) should sit around the outside of the circle, looking in (like a goldfish bowl). As group facilitator you should sit in the centre circle with Group A and ask a question about the community to get the group discussing. Once the discussion takes off, the facilitator should keep quiet. Group B should only listen and observe – they should not speak out their own views. Questions should only be asked in order to draw out the story or views of those in the middle

2. After 10 minutes, the group facilitator should ask Group B to sit in the centre, with Group A looking in. As facilitator, start the discussion asking questions like 'Did they miss out any obvious points?' 'Did they overstate certain issues?' Again, once the discussion has got going, the group facilitator should just observe.

3. After 10 minutes, you may think it appropriate to ask the two groups to swap places again. Group A may want to discuss what they heard Group B talk about, and so on.

4. Once you think the process is running out of steam, bring the discussion to a close and draw out the key points of agreement and disagreement that have been reached about the community. These are points that will be worth exploring with individuals and groups outside your group.

Issue groups? (20 mins)

What

List all the different issues and needs identified by the research and write each one on a piece of paper or Post-It note. Rank these in order of how important each issue was to the people with whom your group talked. What did the majority of people feel was the biggest issue? Compare this with the information you collated prior to the session. See if it tallies with the group feedback.

Agree the four or five major themes which seem to be emerging.

Who

Explain to the group that in order to 'go deeper' during Step Two of the Connection process it will be necessary to focus on these four or five key areas. The best way to do this will be to form small issue groups to look at each one.

> **HELPFUL HINT:**
>
> If you are working with a small group, you have a few options at this stage:
>
> 1. Set aside time as a whole group to research each issue in turn.
>
> 2. Cut your major themes to two or three.
>
> (It may be that your research has revealed only one major issue. If this is the case don't try and force things by struggling to find others – focus on this one issue.)

Your issue groups will take responsibility for identifying key individuals and groups to consult and for listening to their views on the issue. Ask people to choose the issue that most interests them and join that group. Each group should discuss for their issue:

1. What information does the group need to know?

2. Who do they need to talk to?

3. What questions do they need to ask?

4. What skills would be most appropriate?

When

Each issue group should decide which person/s will do what and when. Since the groups will work fairly independently of each other, they will need to choose a co-ordinator who will need to be in regular contact with you as leader, as well as the other issue groups. This way there should be no undue overlap and any information which people feel may be useful to another group can easily be passed on.

It would be good to end with each group giving a quick summary of what they will be doing. This should lend itself naturally to a time of focused prayer.

> **HELPFUL HINT:**
>
> You may like to hand out Information sheets for Step 2 as you did for Step 1 (see Express Together at the end of this chapter).

SESSION 12

LISTEN DEEPER

Step 3 of Connecting within Community

Aim: To provide a simple format to review the findings of Step One of the Connecting process and to prepare the group for Step Three – checking their conclusions.

YOU WILL NEED:

a Bible, A1 paper, A4 paper, pens, Information Summary sheets

HELPFUL HINT:

There will be a big temptation for groups to start talking about solutions. Try to keep them focused on the needs.

The moment of truth (15 mins)

Split into small groups of between four and five (the issue groups would be ideal). Ask each group to write one obscure fact about each individual on a large sheet of paper, plus one fact that isn't true of any of them. After five minutes ask each group to pass their paper to the group on the left, who should then decide which fact relates to which group member and which is untrue.

Issue group feedback (15 mins)

This session is designed to allow each issue group to share the findings from their conversations, group discussions and research during Stage 2: Connecting within Community. First ask each group to list the key issues/points/concerns/needs they have identified, and put them in order of importance. They should discuss and agree upon what they see as the main conclusions to be drawn from their research into this particular issue. They should write these down on a large sheet of paper, e.g. 'The biggest issues facing the elderly in this community are ...' They may find it useful to use the 'But why ... ?' mode of questioning as a way of checking their initial conclusions. Alternatively you may choose to do this as a whole group once the smaller groups have reported back some of their findings.

But why? (20 mins)

'But why?' flow charts are a way of helping people to think about the root causes of problems they encounter. It takes people away from superficial answers that scrape the surface to more fundamental issues. When used in the context of an interview it is also a good way of challenging the assumptions and prejudices of the interviewers themselves. Simply asking 'But why?' all the time may be perceived as somewhat confrontational so it may be worth explaining the approach before you do it. In an interview situation it may be worth jotting down their answer, asking a few other questions around that issue, and then asking the next 'But why?' question, so that not every question is the same.

IN AN INTERVIEW CONTEXT

1. Ask the individual or group to identify a problem in their community. Draw or write the issue in a box at the top of the page.

2. Then ask: 'But why has this happened?' The participants write their response in another box and draw a line connecting the two. Again ask the question, 'But why has this happened?' Gradually a flow chart is built up going back to the root causes.

3. Use the completed flow chart as a basis for further discussion. You could ask questions like:

- Which of the causes that you have listed do you think are most important?
- Which of the causes you have listed do you think you can change?
- Which of the causes you have listed do you think the community could work together in changing?

For the purpose of this session, encourage each group to take one of the issues they have identified as an area of need in their community, such as homelessness among teenagers, or more specifically to address the needs of a particular homeless teenager, and then to ask themselves the question, 'Why is the person like this?' After each answer, encourage them to ask again: 'But why?' and to keep asking the question until they have got as far as they think they can go. For example:

The teenager is homeless
↓
But why?
↓
Because she hated her mum's new boyfriend
↓
But why?
↓
Because he kept hitting her and her mum
↓
But why?
↓
Because he drank too much
↓
But why?
↓
Because he lost his job, etc.

You may find that some are more complicated, and could be best represented through a more complex flow chart, for example:

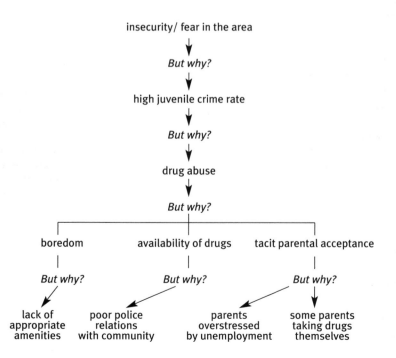

insecurity/ fear in the area
↓
But why?
↓
high juvenile crime rate
↓
But why?
↓
drug abuse
↓
But why?

| boredom | availability of drugs | tacit parental acceptance |

But why?   *But why?*   *But why?*

| lack of appropriate amenities | poor police relations with community | parents overstressed by unemployment | some parents taking drugs themselves |

If you chosen to do the 'But why?' exercise in issue groups ask each group to take it in turn to present the diagrams and to answer questions. This process will help each group be critical of the thinking behind their conclusions. As leader, draw out any common themes.

● ●

Giants vs the Saints (20 mins)

Phrase 2 of *Express Community* may have taken some time and at this point you may feel like you are approaching something significant. However, what you consider to be true about a people group, issue or place may still be quite subjective. What people consider to be true or not depends on their own experience of the past, their understanding of the present and their perception of what lies in front of them. Reflect on Numbers 13:16-33 together, and ask yourself:

● What are the 'giants' you feel you may be about to face in your own community? Why?

● In what ways might it be valuable to check these out again?

● In what ways might checking your initial conclusions at this stage help to prevent Numbers 14:1-4 moments?

● At this stage do you have any sense of what the 'milk and honey' might be like for your community?

Perhaps spend a moment reflecting on the following poem by Stewart Henderson[4]:

LAND OF MILK AND HONEY

Is this the land of milk and honey?
The one for which this city give
conscripted youth to War's dark waters,
Woodbind battalions of the brave.
This city of abandoned vehicles,
bankrupt stock and playtime crack.
Promised land of little promise,
a gaunt consumer cul-de-sac.

When we were young, Orwell, Priestley,
chastened us with post cards home
writing of a TB kingdom,
a cloth capped land of monochrome.
And as for their HP descendants
cocooned in space with Satellite,
not knowing of the word redemption,
owned by the loan shark's knock at night.

Is this the land of milk and honey
where birdsong seldom cleans the air?
And all around is glass confetti

and only strangers pause to stare.
Absorbed into the locals' spirits,
demons of despondency,
souls and bodies soaked in debt
crying out for Jubilee.

Yet Heaven lingers in these side streets,
amidst the metal shutter shops
where lethal games played with syringes
have long replaced kid's spinning tops.
And Heaven lodges in these side streets
feeling each tormenting pain,
swallowing each tranquilliser,
visiting the barely sane.

This is a land of milk and honey,
and perpetual alarms,
full of light and sawn-off menace,
a daily paradox of psalms.
This is the land of milk and honey,
bereft of bud and bursting leaves,
though glory may not seem apparent
– a place where Jesus lives and breaths.

At this point of great potential it is still important that you take time to check out your conclusions about the needs in your community. This way you will have done all you can to ensure that your community is able to discover what 'milk and honey' might taste like for them. You may feel as though you are beginning to understand what Jesus ruling in the midst of chaos and need might look like, but you may also be feeling overwhelmed at the enormity of the task. Don't let this feeling obscure your vision and prevent you seeing it happen. Now is the time to remember who it is that has called you to begin to express community, how he got you to this point and the fact that he is with you. Who can be against you, providing you stick with his purposes!

• •

What happens next? (20 mins)

In issue groups, ask people to amend their conclusions in the light of their discussions. Ask them to discuss their ideas for who they should check their conclusions with (including local people they have already talked to and key gatekeepers). The group should agree how they will do this and what further questions they will want to ask. One of the key questions they will want to ask is how to go about responding to the needs identified. The issue group agrees who will do what. Each issue group then gives a quick summary of what they will be doing in Step 3 of Connecting within Community.

HELPFUL HINT:

You may like to hand out Information sheets for Step 3 as you did for Steps 1 and 2 (see p. 139).

EXPRESS TOGETHER

PEOPLE WORTH LISTENING TO

Age groups in the community

children, teenagers, young adults, 25-55-year-olds, early retirees, elderly people

Community groups

sport clubs, political associations, local residents' associations, voluntary organisations, the Women's Institute, youth clubs, parent and toddler groups

Religious groups

other churches, mosques, Hindu temples, synagogues

Gatekeepers

CRIME

community police, local Neighbourhood Watch committee member

EDUCATION

pre-school children's workers, teachers, school governors, education welfare officers

EMPLOYMENT

Job Centre managers, Social Security officers, local employers, school career advisers, unemployed people

FAMILIES UNDER STRESS

Citizens Advice Bureau debt counsellors, Relate marriage counsellors, shopkeepers, social workers

HEALTH

social services, local GPs, local mental health organisations, local hospitals, people with mental health problems

HOMELESSNESS

shelter workers, homeless people, local authority housing officers

RECREATION

leisure centre managers, publicans, betting shop managers, social club committee members

STEP 1

Information summary (to be used during or after each individual or group discussion).

A. Background

1. Your name

2. Issue/theme being researched

3. Who did you talk to? *(e.g. doctor, local resident, etc.)*

4. Which skill did you use? *(e.g. chatting, group discussion, mapping, etc.)*

5. If your research involved a group, how many people were there?

6. If your research involved a group, give the age range:
   Age: 6-12 13-18 19-30 31-45 46-60 61-75 76+

7. If your research involved a group, give the ratio of men to women:
   Gender: Male   Female

8. Where did the individual/group members live *(or work, if more relevant)*?

B. Key information gathered

1. What did the individual/group think was positive about the community?

2. What did the individual/group think was negative about the community?

3. What did the individual/group think were the most important issues in the community?

4. Who did the individual/group think were the people with the biggest needs in the community?

5. What would the individual/group most like to see changed in the community?

6. What other significant comments did the individual/group make?

7. Are there any comments or observations you would like to make?

8. Would the individual/group be interested in finding out the results of this survey?
   Yes   No   Not sure   *(If 'yes', please give their address.)*

9. Would this be a good individual/group to talk to further about these issues?
   Yes   No

STEP 2

Information summary (to be used during or after each individual or group discussion).

A. Background

1. Your name

2. Issue/theme being researched

3. Who did you talk to? *(e.g. doctor, local resident, etc.)*

4. Which skill did you use? *(e.g. chatting, group discussion, mapping, etc.)*

5. If your research involved a group, how many people were there?

6. If your research involved a group, give the age range:
   Age: 6-12 13-18 19-30 31-45 46-60 61-75 76+

7. If your research involved a group, give ratio of men to women:
   Gender: Male   Female

8. Where did the individual/group members live *(or work, if more relevant)*?

B. Key information gathered

1. Did the individual/group think the issue/theme was significant in the community?
   Yes   No   What reasons were given?

2. What did the individual/group think was the impact of the issue on the community?

3. What did the individual/group think were the main causes of the issue?

4. In what ways is the issue already being addressed?

5. Did the individual/group make any suggestions for how they thought these issues could be addressed?

6. What other significant comments did the individual/group make?

7. Are there any comments or observations you would like to make?

8. Would this individual/group be interested in finding out the results of this survey?
   Yes   No   Not sure   *(If 'yes', please give their address.)*

9. Would this be a good individual/group to talk to further about these issues?
   Yes   No

STEP 3

Information summary (to be used during or after each individual or group discussion).

A. Background

1. Your name

2. Issue/theme being researched

3. Who did you talk to? *(e.g. doctor, local resident, etc.)*

4. Which skill did you use? *(e.g. chatting, group discussion, mapping, etc.)*

5. If your research involved a group, how many people were there?

6. If your research involved a group, give the age range:
   Age: 6-12 13-18 19-30 31-45 46-60 61-75 76+

7. If your research involved a group, give ratio of men/women:
   Gender: Male Female

8. Where did the individual/group members live *(or work, if more relevant)*?

B. Key information gathered

1. Did the individual/group agree with the conclusions of the Stage 2 review meeting?
   Yes   No   What reasons were given?

2. In what ways is the issue already being addressed?

3. Did the individual/group make any suggestions for how they thought these issues could be addressed?

4. What other significant comments did the individual/group make?

5. Are there any comments or observations you would like to make?

6. Would this individual/group be interested in finding out the results of this survey? Yes   No   Not sure   *(If 'yes', please give their address.)*

7. Would this be a good individual/group to talk to further about these issues?
   Yes   No

8. Would the individual/group be interested in helping out if your group decided to get involved in this issue?

1 The actual title was: "Why Don't You Just Switch Off Your Television Set And Go Out And Do Something Less Boring Instead?" Various groups of kids, e.g. The Belfast Gang, The Birmingham Gang, would arrive every school holidays to suggest things which might be less boring than watching TV. Of course, if the programme had actually succeeded then it wouldn't have had an audience.

2 A. Huczynski and D. Buchanan, *Organisational Behaviour: An Introductory Text*, 5th edition (Edinburgh: Pearson Education Ltd, 2004), p. 739.

3 Adapted from Michael Puffet and Sheldon W. Rottler, *Red Hot Ice Breakers* (London: Monarch Books, 1999), p. 49.

4 Copyright © Stewart Henderson 1997. From the poetry collection *Limited Edition* published by Plover Books. Used with the author's permission. All rights reserved.

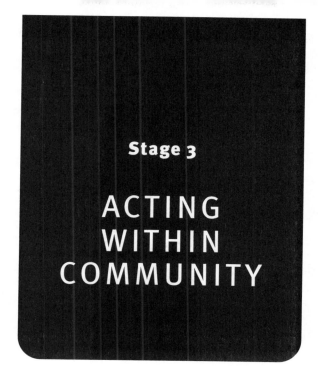

Stage 3

ACTING
WITHIN
COMMUNITY

You did not **choose** me, but I chose you and appointed you to go and **bear fruit**- fruit that will **last** (Jn. 15:16).

Chapter 5

A VISION OF INTIMACY

By now you must be desperate to get going, but at this point, just as in the previous stages, it is crucial that you resist diving in and doing something that is potentially inappropriate in the community. All your hard work so far could be undone. You need to listen to God just as carefully here as you have at any other stage. You may already have ideas about what you'd like to see happen in your community; this chapter will help you to formulate some of these into a long-term vision for your group. There is more to finding your vision than debates, diagrams and decisions, however: you and your group will need to be creative about the ways in which you allow space and time to develop an intimate relationship with your God as well as your community.

WHO: BELIEVING *YOU* ARE CHOSEN!

What is your lasting memory of break-time at school? It will probably depend on your age and maybe even your ability to remember that far back, but it might be things like free milk, kiss chase, fish-and-chip-flavoured crisps, swapping stickers on the yard, or perhaps that dreaded moment when someone suggests it would be a good idea to pick teams. No matter what the sport or game – hockey, netball, basketball, football or even cowboys and Indians – picking teams was always inevitable, if not at first break certainly at dinnertime. The method and the torture were always the same. Standing against the wall, your fate in the hands of some self-appointed captain. Slowly the number of people standing against the wall shrinks, and as the two teams grow, you and a few others are left wondering whether you are going to be last or not. Even when picking numbers became the new fashion, things were not improved because even if you were picked first it never felt as though you were being chosen because you were you. Picking numbers simply left you full of doubt as to whether you were actually wanted or not. Of course even the apparently flawless process of picking numbers eventually got corrupted as those in the know developed sophisticated codes to ensure they got picked first, like coughing once if they were number one or scratching their head twice for number two or 'Captain, *please, please, please*, pick me' (i.e. 'I'm number three!'). You really knew you weren't wanted when the captains decided it was time to renumber everyone and pick again.

Thankfully, as John 15:16 points out, we have a God who says, 'I choose you.' Whether we always hear him or not is another matter, but it's the truth. Regardless of whether we feel worthy or not, it is his last word on the subject. He wants you because you are you, not because of what you are not. You would do well to remember this as you consider your role within this Express Community process.

WHAT FOR: TO DO SOMETHING

Whilst it is true that we were chosen for no other reason than God's desire to have a relationship with us, it is equally true that there is a point to that relationship. Jesus says in John 15:16 that his disciples (and as his followers we can assume that this applies to us also) have been 'appointed' – but why and what for? To be appointed means to be recognised, to be given some kind of responsibility because we have something to offer or do. In order to know what that is, you need to know God intimately. You are chosen for a job or a role because something you have makes you suitable for the task.

The word 'bear' in verse 15 is significant. 'You did not choose me, but I chose you and appointed you to go and bear fruit' (Jn. 15:16). This suggests that God believes you have the potential to do something productive and beneficial for the sake of others. Be assured by his having chosen you, by his having loved you enough to want to include you, by his affirmation of your potential, and by his commitment to be 'at work within us' (Eph 3:20), but be challenged also. Bearing something takes effort: hard work.

People generally respond to responsibility/recognition in two ways. You are either the type of person who will rise to the challenge or run from it. You will either doubt your ability, skills and talents or have overwhelming faith in yourself. Either you approach mornings with the attitude, 'Hello, world, it's good to see you. What are we going to accomplish today?' or 'Oh, it's not that time already, is it? Perhaps just another five minutes in bed ...' Many within your group may feel the same way.

WHY ME?

Most of us, if we are honest, have a low opinion of ourselves and our own ability. Express Community as a process may have given your group some confidence, particularly as they've begun to connect with people during Stage Two, but as the moment of truth gets ever closer, when you might actually have to do something active, you will slowly begin to see doubt rearing its ugly head. More often than not, as soon as someone has faith in an individual, they react by losing all faith in themselves: 'I couldn't possibly;' 'No, not me;' or 'Isn't there someone else?' You can probably think of occasions yourself when you have asked someone capable to do something, but were surprised when they responded with a 'no way'. Maybe that was your response when someone asked you! Just look at Moses' response to his appointment in Exodus 4:1. People begin to forget why God chose them and look at the gifts others have rather than seeing the potential destiny in their own hands. At that point you need to remember, and probably your group need to be reminded, that you have been *chosen*, simply because you are you, and *appointed*, simply because you are you!

Back to those fruits again. The thing about fruit trees is that they are always fruit trees, even when they are seeds, shoots or stems. Though they may not bear fruit initially, they always have the potential: they may simply need to grow a bit first before they are ready. The Bible is full of examples of people who doubted themselves or were doubted by others. None seemed good enough, but God used them anyway: they realised their potential. David the brave leader of a nation was just as brave, but on a smaller scale, when he was a leader of sheep. Paul the enthusiastic, energetic apostle was just as passionate when he was a Jew trying to kill Christians. The gifts were there, they just needed to grow in the direction that God intended. The question is: what sort of fruit is God calling you to bear in your community – what is your calling or purpose, as individuals and as a group – and how do you find that out?

HOW TO LOVE: YOUR CALLING

'This is my command: Love each other.' This is Jesus' final word to his disciples in John 15:17. How you choose to do that is your call! As you begin to explore what it is that God is calling you to do in your community, it will be easy to get sucked into all kinds of structures, equations and processes. This is totally appropriate and the Express Community process will actively encourage this. We are not called to run aimlessly or beat the air (1 Cor. 9:26). However, as Christians seeking to express community, it is crucial that at all times you keep your God in focus. At the beginning of this process we talked about the need to see through Jesus' integral mission to his motivation. It was shaped by who he was, i.e. his identity in God and his lifestyle choices: what he did, i.e. his choice to love others, and why – his love for God. This gives us some idea about what is required of us if we are to understand how we should bring *Express Community* to its natural conclusion, as an integral mission that involves us thoroughly living within community.

At the heart of *Express Community* is the belief that we love people and serve them for Christ's sake and that our deepest desire is to see people finding fullness of life in Jesus. It is going to take a considerable amount of spiritual energy to live as a Christian in the service of the community. For this very reason, the whole Express Community process is as much about spiritual strength as it is about seeking to serve. No real progress will be made without utter dependence on God and much prayer. Remember back to Chapter 1 where we talked about a desire for people in our community to become members of the kingdom both now and in the future. Your ability to recognise needs, restore needs and to offer people opportunities to return to God is dependent on the degree to which you are aware of God's will. This means being close enough to him to hear his whispers above the other louder demands on our time and energy.

It is easy when we start talking about things such as 'life calling' or 'ministry' to miss the opportunities in front of our noses. God desires us to be faithful in the day of small things as much as, and possibly more than, in the grander things (Zech. 4:10). In the Bible God offers a range of callings: micro for the short term, macro for the long term and somewhere in between, the intermediate, which represents a kind of 'middle-term' phase of life. All of these will be significant as you seek to serve your community and as you seek to live a life worthy of God's calling (2 Thes. 1:11).

MACRO VISION – *WHY* YOU NEED TO KNOW

Our focus tends to be on the spectacular rather than the ordinary. The kind of macro questions we might ask ourselves are, 'What do I do with the rest of my life?' or the childlike statements God encourages such as, 'When I grow up I'm going to be a ...'

There are many ways to discover this kind of vision. Most of us would probably like a neon sign like Moses or Paul (Ex. 3; Acts 9:2-4), but there are others. Sometimes God uses someone else to give us this vision, as in the story of Samuel and David (1 Sam. 16:1-13). Sometimes we grow into a role, like Joshua or Timothy (Joshua's skills are recognised in Deut. 1:37-39 but not commissioned until Deut. 31:6-8; 14-15).

The problem is that when we talk and think about calling or purpose in this way we immediately begin to think of the long-term future and forget what is going on in the present.

INTERMEDIATE VISION/CALLING – *WHAT* YOU NEED TO DO

The reality is that the only way to play with a long-term vision is by aiming in the correct direction and scoring short-term goals! That is why the strategic Session plans 13–15, which form part of this Stage, and the conclusion are crucial to any attempt to live with purpose. Calling is as much about the next minute, hour, day and the coming week, as it is about next year. It is important to remember this when we begin to express community. Maybe you have not even considered your 'life calling' but you have probably thought about what you might do next year – about a holiday, a new car or a new job maybe?

Somewhere in the middle of macro and micro calling which we'll consider next are all those questions about what to do during this or that time of my life. There is of course nothing wrong with planning; but what about this year? You see the trap we all fall into is focusing too far ahead and missing what's under our nose. Eating the main course while looking at the sweet menu. Renting a video or DVD and fast-forwarding to the end to see what happens.

MICRO VISION/CALLING – *WHO* YOU NEED TO BE

God's got something for you in the next 30 seconds – jump too far ahead and you might miss something significant! Micro vision is all about now and what next. It may not sound as grand but it is no less significant. Joseph and Mary were prevented from returning to Egypt at the last minute (Mt. 2:13-15). Paul was stopped from going to Bithynia (Acts 16:6-10). Maxine, a girl whose team I was privileged to be a part of during a mission in Sparkbrook, Birmingham, would ask God what she should say every time she approached someone or someone approached her. Try it: you'll speak to more people than you ever thought possible about things you never thought possible! We may have our life all mapped out, but we need to remain flexible to God's calling in micro situations. We need to be open to his call at any minute and be able to change tack at very short notice. Any journey starts with small steps; if you want to discover your calling for life, start by asking God what to do in the next five minutes! If you want to know what it is you should be doing in your community, ask God to reveal what he wants you to say to the next person you meet.

This type of vision, micro, is what *Express Community* has been all about. It's about knowing God's vision for the here and now, allowing his calling to guide the choices you make day in, day out. That is what made Jesus' mission so successful, so integral. *Express Community* has encouraged you to use structured steps, but there will come a time when it should become second nature. In reality we need all three types of vision in order to understand how we are to live more effectively within community. We need to know who we need to be, what we need to do and why we need to do it. The only way to discover your vision or calling for life is to understand what steps you must take in order to get into a position where you can hear God clearly. The most important thing is time. Not time doing nothing, but time doing something important – striving for intimacy with God. There is no substitute for

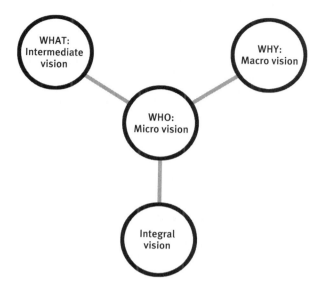

spending time getting to know God; we often call it 'quiet time' but 'quality time' is probably more accurate because if it is working it should be anything but quiet – you should be hearing God! You should be constantly engaged in discipleship with him, recognising you are chosen, communicating through prayer and devotion, being committed to Jesus, changing through the Spirit and practising compassion for others through community with others. For an effective life in community you'll need to find ways for you and your group, individually and corporately, to develop a pattern of living that promotes intimacy above all else. Intimacy with God may look something like this:

THE CYCLE OF INTIMACY

KNOWING *WHO* GOD IS CALLING YOU TO BE

Relationship

Like any relationship, intimacy begins by simply agreeing to meet with God – a kind of 'let's do lunch', or 'let's go out and see if we get on'. Initially this happens when you first become a Christian, but as you grow and develop it will be appropriate to ask the question again and again. The good thing is that unlike that killer moment when you fear whether the other person will say yes or no, God won't reject you. Often he makes the first move, hence, 'I chose you' (Jn. 15:16).

Familiarity

To be familiar with God means knowing him and being known by him. It is about being at ease in his presence, comfortable and yet not complacent. God knows everything there is to know about you (Ps. 139), but in order for you to begin to be familiar with him, you need to ask him to reveal things to you about his character, nature and personality.

KNOWING *WHAT* GOD IS CALLING YOU TO DO

Recognition

If you know someone well it is easy to recognise him or her. If you have ever lost a friend shopping or at the football match somehow you can manage to pick them out of a crowd by their hairstyle, their walk or their voice. Israel missed Jesus' birth, misjudging his life and misunderstanding his death. God told them what to look for, but they still missed all the signs. They knew the law inside out, but missed it completely because they did not have that intimate relationship with God. Recognition is more than simply knowing the facts about someone; it's about a much deeper connection.

Closeness

To be close means to be in a place where you can hear God's words and know when it is he who is directing thoughts, words and actions – even in the busyness of community life.

KNOWING *WHY* GOD IS CALLING TO YOU

Understanding

Closeness brings an understanding of why things go a certain way and why sometimes they don't. If God is love then he is always love, even when we don't think he is, i.e. when things are difficult or hard. He doesn't change; we do. It takes intimate understanding to know why things happen as they do.

Confidence

Intimacy with God brings a new understanding of God's plan/guidance and a confidence that releases us to 'have a go'. It acts as a kind of safety net. Confidence comes from knowing that God will always be there even when we fall or fail. Confidence brings trust: God has been there in the past, he will be there in the future. Whatever you have discovered about *why* God has called you as a result of *Express Community* it is important to understand that a basic trust in him should inform the decisions you make in every area of your life and not just within your community. Trust is the basis of any relationship, which brings us back full circle to where we started.

KEY QUESTIONS:

Prayer, reading the Bible, spending time with God and allowing the Holy Spirit to work in your life are the things that make the circle we talk about above complete. They are the things required for true intimacy. Building these things into everything you do will be the key to your ability to express community.

- What stage are you at in the cycle of intimacy?
- Do you feel as though you are in God's circle of intimacy at this moment?
- What about your group?
- How do you need to be in order to live effectively in your community?

ENGAGE YOUR GROUP

The following sessions are designed to introduce people to the principles of developing a strategy, which for some may be a relatively new concept. You could choose to use them over a period of weeks, days, a weekend or just a day. Use the schedule opposite as a guide to your planning:

OPTION A: TWO DAYS (SEPARATE OR A WEEKEND)

Day 1

Session 13:	10.00 – 10.30
Part A:	10.30 – 11.00
Break	
Part B:	11.30 – 12.00
Part C:	12.30 – 13.00
Lunch	
Express together:	13.30 – 14.00

Day 2

Session 14:	09.30 – 10.30
Part A:	10.30 – 11.00
Break	
Part B:	11.30 – 12.00
Part C:	12.30 – 13.00
Lunch	
Express together:	13.30 – 14.00

OPTION B: ONE DAY

Session 13:	09.30 – 10.00
Part A:	10.00 – 10.30
Break	
Part B:	11.00 – 11.30
Part C:	11.30 – 12.30
Lunch	
Express together:	13.00 – 13.30
Session 14:	13.30 – 14.30
Part A:	14.30 – 15.00
Break	
Part B:	15.30 – 16.00
Part C:	16.00 – 16.30
Express together:	16.30 – 17.00

OPTION C: INDIVIDUAL SESSIONS

Use each part as an individual session to explore over the next six weeks.

SESSION 13

ISSUES (30 MINS)

YOU WILL NEED:

paper, pens or pencils

You will probably have divided people into groups at the second stage of the listening and information-gathering process, when you were encouraging them to focus on five or six key themes. These groups may provide the best structure for the feeding back of information. It is recommended that these groups meet prior to the workshop to prepare a presentation of their findings on their particular issue. They should be encouraged to present the results of their research in a creative way (such as using drama, telling stories or using photographs) and then to summarise their key points at the end. Allow time at the end of each presentation for people to ask questions.

SESSION 13 (PART A)

SYMPTOMS (30 MINS)

YOU WILL NEED:

paper, coloured pens, Post-it notes

Problem tree

Divide people into different groups and ask them to produce a 'problem tree' for each issue, reflecting on what they have heard from the presentation. You may need to allocate a specific issue to each group and to ensure that there is at least one member of the group who was involved in researching that particular issue. In the groups, discuss some of the *symptoms* that influence this need. These can be shown in the form of a tree (see opposite), with the symptoms being the leaves and branches (which are visible). For example, if the group were looking at the issue of isolation in elderly people, some of the symptoms may be loneliness, poor diet or lack of social interaction. The 'problem tree' is like the activity 'But why?' from Session 12, but it will eventually move on to look at a wider range of factors that influence the problem, including:

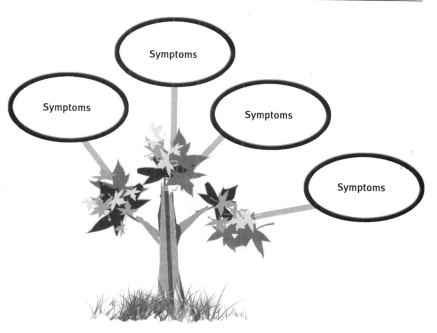

Step 1: Symptoms

Step 2: Causes

Step 3: Solutions

This can be a very helpful way of analysing an issue. Stick the groups' problem trees on the wall and encourage people to go and look at them.

SESSION 13 (PART B)

CAUSES (30 MINS)

YOU WILL NEED:

paper, coloured pens, Post-it notes

Remaining in the same groups, add to the tree by brainstorming some of the causes of those symptoms. These can be added to the 'tree' as roots below the ground (since they are not always visible). If the group were looking at the issue of isolation in elderly people, some of the causes may be families living too far away to visit, poor public transport, fear of being mugged if people go outside.

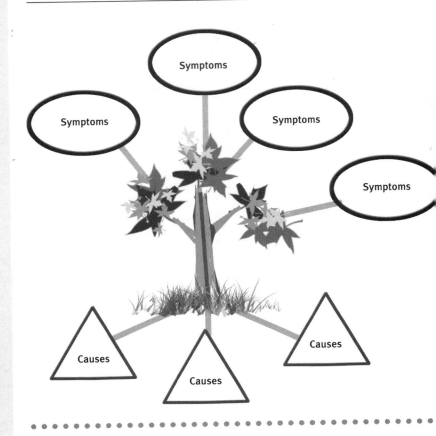

Ranking

Ask the group to rank the causes according to how significant they seemed to be from the research they carried out during Stage Two: Connecting within Community.

SESSION 13 (PART C)

SOLUTIONS (30 MINS)

Now add possible responses or *solutions* to the tree. Remain in the same groups. Give each group one of the problem trees and encourage them to come up with responses that will address a key cause or significant symptom of the problem. Feed in any ideas that people in the community were suggesting. Other agencies will undoubtedly have already recognised, and be working towards solving, some of the symptoms and root causes of the issues you have identified. Add their names to the tree too. You should by now be fully aware of who is doing what in your community from your research during Stage Two: Connecting with Community. Before starting this exercise, you may want to establish some ground rules, such as the following:

1. Any idea goes, no matter how small, big, crazy ... or sensible!

2. Don't discuss ideas in depth.

3. We're not looking for specific projects at this stage, but simple actions.

After about seven minutes, rotate the problem tree diagrams. This way each group will start to consider their response to a different issue, but with the benefit of the first group's ideas as a basis.

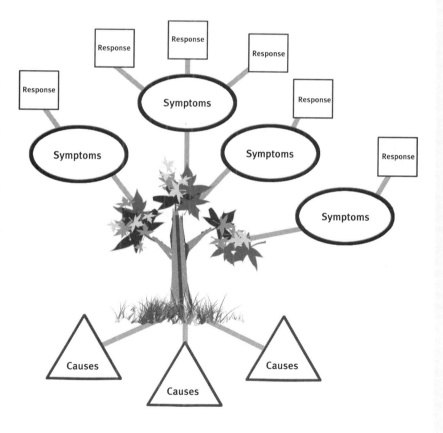

EXPRESS TOGETHER

SITUATION, MISSION AND AIMS (30 MINS)

Transfer the information from your tree diagrams to the grid below.

Produce one for each issue.

	A		B
Issue #1	*Enter the name of the issue.*	**Situation**	*Explain how this issue presents itself in your community.*
Symptoms	*List the symptoms from your tree.*	**Mission**	*List your solutions in response to these symptoms.*
Causes	*List the causes from your tree.*	**Aims**	*List your solutions in response to these causes.*

You should now have a completed grid for each of your four different issues, for example:

	A		B
Issue #1	e.g. isolation of elderly people	Situation	e.g. live in a community where the elderly feel isolated
Symptoms	e.g. loneliness, poor diet, lack of social interaction	Mission	e.g. reduce loneliness, provide better diets, increase their interaction
Causes	e.g. families living too far away, poor public transport, fear of being mugged	Aims	e.g. increasing connections with their family, more and better transport, safer place

For each issue you have identified you should now be able to complete the following statements:

1. Situation

We live in a community where the issue of _____ is a particular need.

2. Mission

In response to this we believe we are being called to _____

3. Aims

We aim to meet the need by _____

For example:

---

1. Situation

We live in a community where the issue of isolated elderly people is a particular need.

2. Mission

In response to this we believe we are being called to reduce loneliness, provide better diets and increase elderly people's interaction with others.

3. Aims

We aim to meet the need by strengthening connections with their family, improving transport and making the community a safer place for them.

Saying it all in one go may help to make it sound more real. Try it and see how it feels:

MISSION STATEMENT #1

We live in a community where the issue of *isolated elderly people* is a particular need. In response to this we believe we are being called to *reduce loneliness, provide better diets and increase their interaction with others.* We aim to meet the need by *strengthening connections with their family, improving transport and making the community a safer place for them.*

• •

Ranking

It is important that before you move on to the next stage you focus down even further. What will be the issue you decide to tackle?

Hand out the issue statements and ask people to vote on which one they feel would most meet the needs. Useful questions might be:

● Will the issue help us live out our mission as a group?
● Will the issue meet the needs identified?
● Will the issue benefit those most in need?
● Will the issue get the community involved?
● Is the issue realistic in terms of its demands on group members' time, energy and resources?

You could choose to do this activity within:

- your group
- the wider church
- your community
- or specific community groups

You may need to take a break to consider this.

'Then we will no longer be infants, tossed back and forth by the waves, and blown here and there by every wind of teaching and by the cunning and craftiness of men in their deceitful scheming. Instead, speaking the truth in love, we will in all things grow up into him who is the Head, that is, Christ. From him the whole body, joined and held together by every supporting ligament, grows and builds itself up in love, as each part does its work' (Eph. 4:14-16).

Chapter 6

IDEAS UNLIMITED

'When I grow up I want to be a firefighter!' Or at least that's what my son (aged four) thinks. Who knows? He might well be. For you it could just as easily have been a train driver, a policewoman or, my personal preference, a racing car driver. Perhaps it is still your dream; you are just looking for an opportunity. We all have dreams, especially early on in our lives. Can you remember yours? Sadly, for one reason or another, most of us never quite get there. Most of the time, as part of growing up, you begin to realise that you just weren't being realistic or your passion then is not your passion now. And that's OK! As you set off on this Express Community process many months ago, who would have thought you would get as far as Stage Three? Are the dreams you had then anything like the ones you feel God's calling you to accomplish now? Hopefully your vision of community will have developed as God has given insight about your community through each stage of the process and, as you have grown together as a group, you will have realised what it is that God wants you to do.

As you have reflected and connected within your community during Stages One to Two of your journey, your strength as a group will have been the major reason why you have been able to resist being blown off course. As you face the conclusion of Stage Three and begin to consider how you might shape your method of Acting within Community, you will find that in order for your integral mission to remain long term you may have to grow again. As this chapter progresses you may feel that it is time to start seeing yourself more as a team than as a group. What's the difference, you ask? A leader I know once described it this way:

	GROUP	TEAM
Purpose	Be	Do
Action	Be more and do less	Do more and be less
Aims	Don't have to get on	Need to be looking in the same direction
Leadership style	Don't need a leader	Captain/leader
Atmosphere	Sometimes non-cooperation, sometimes cooperation	Should be about cooperation
Skills, interests, gifts	Similar skills and similar interests	Different skills and different interests

GROWING INDIVIDUALS: THE DISCIPLE CYCLE

If Jesus, co-creator of the universe, saw the importance of working as a team at creation and of investing in team at incarnation, what leader could construct an argument that suggested otherwise? Despite all his credentials, Jesus never used his immediate resources to bring immediate glory to himself in the short term, instead choosing to invest his energy in building a team for the long term. He used his presence to model a life that would train others to carry on his work in the future. In effect his job was to do himself out of a job: a great developmental principle if ever there was one! In a similar way, whatever way you choose to facilitate team, your group should never feel that you as leader are not there for them when they need you. We as Christians are not left high and dry. Jesus does not wind us up like a clockwork toy and leave us to run down: along with his great commission comes his great promise, that he will be with us always, 'to the very end of the age' (Mt. 28:19-20). God will always be there for you and your team.

As well as preaching, teaching and healing, Jesus saw spending a considerable amount time with just 12 men as an integral part of his mission to the whole world. He also saw the potential and significance of three of those 12 (Peter, James and John), which is why he invested so much time with them.[1] Jesus chose to take the power he had at his disposal and release it, in order to release others to give to others – a great model of empowerment, straight from the top! In Luke 10 we see Jesus appointing 72 others to go out and continue what he had begun to model through his own life and mission (Lk. 10:1-2; 16-18). Jesus was the model leader, trusting his team and allowing them to learn on the job (Lk. 9:1-9). His model was simple:

- Watch what I do.
- Do it while I watch you.
- Do it on your own.
- Let someone watch you do it.

However you go about building team or working with others, you would do well to apply some of these principles to your own work. When involved in community work or in tackling injustice, we need to remember Jesus' example of including others. He encouraged people to get involved from the start, allowed them to make mistakes and supported their growth. He used an eclectic mix of ideas, initiatives and individual styles, skills and specialisms that he found in the resources around him (Lk. 5:1-11).

GROWING YOUR GROUP INTO A TEAM

Each team will have individual needs. The best way to find out what will keep your team going is to ask them! Ask your group to list all the things they feel would restrict a team working, the things to avoid. Maybe you have experienced some already, or there may be things you think might be a problem if you worked together more: be honest. Finish on a high note; list the things they feel would contribute to making teamwork work. The things your group say will affect your role as team leader. At times you will find it hard to get the balance right between meeting the needs of your team and meeting the needs of your community. However, if you want your integral mission to have life, then it is a balance that you are going to have to manage well. Ephesians 4:14-16 contains seven important verbs (i.e. 'doing' words) for creating an effective team:

1. Joining – A team needs to have a sense of belonging, welcome and warmth.

2. Holding – The group must provide a place to feel safe and secure.

3. Supporting – Members must support each other: both the leaders and the rest of the team.

4. Growing – The team must make room for personal and inner growth, perhaps growth that could not happen in another context.

5. Building – This is about corporate growth, building together, growing together, challenging one another and striving to be better.

6. Loving – An effective team will teach it members to be selfless – doing what another person wants/needs despite our own feelings.

7. Working – A team is a team primarily in order to work. Hard work through cooperation offers a sense of achievement.

Getting the balance right between getting the task done and supporting your team will be tricky. Too much support and people may begin to feel smothered, too little and they may feel isolated. Too much focusing on the task will cause people either to rise to it or run from it. The following diagram may help you to visualise how 'support versus challenge' affects your group as individuals. You might like to plot the four extremes and then ask your group for a range of emotions and experiences they might feel in those situations. It may give you useful insight into what your leadership needs to provide.

HIGH CHALLENGE	
stressed swamped deserted isolated exposed lonely	excited enthusiastic proud fulfilled motivated encouraged valued
LOW SUPPORT	**HIGH SUPPORT**
lack of: encouragement resources funding training monitoring evaluation	frustrated comfortable hindered bored wasted smothered
LOW CHALLENGE	

GROWING TEAM

One of the simplest and yet most profound understandings of the meaning of 'team' is: Together Everyone Achieves More. There are many strengths in working as a team in partnership with other individuals. For example, teams can:

- support each other
- offer a variety of different ideas, gifts and skills
- offer increased vision
- provide for greater accountability
- share the workload
- develop trust

Of course, where there is strength there is always weakness. Team brings out the worst in people as well as the best. For example, teams can experience:

- conflict
- disappointment
- unhealthy reliance on others
- suspicion
- adverse effects of having individuals' weaknesses highlighted
- conflict between different agendas

At a training session in the south-west of England, some of the leaders were quite honest about why they thought teamwork was tough, and why some chose to avoid it. The result was the following:

EXPRESS EXPERIENCE

- **Ability.** Some members of the team are not up to the task.
- **Battles.** Working with people means arguments and disagreement.
- **Control.** Some of us as leaders are afraid of losing it.
- **Delegation.** It can take forever to ask someone else to do something; often it's quicker to do it yourself.
- **Energy.** A lot of energy is spent on the team that would be better directed into the task.
- **Fear.** My own personal weaknesses as leader will be more obvious as someone in the group may be better than me.
- **Glory.** Working with others deflects attention from my own achievements.
- **Hurts.** Trusting people in the past has resulted in upset and pain.
- **Inflexibility.** It takes longer to change things when you have to take a whole number of people with you.
- **Judged.** My every action, decision, suggestion as leader is open to criticism.

It may be a useful exercise to encourage your group to attempt to come up with an A-Z of why team is good. Despite the fact that many leaders struggle with team and many teams struggle with leaders, most would admit that working together adds something dynamic to any task. Doing things together is so much more fun: why else would we choose to pay money to watch films at the cinema together, or gather around the world's smallest portable TV to watch big sporting occasions in the company of others, or travel miles to meet up with colleagues, family or friends for Christmas, birthdays and New Year?

Your ability to express community will depend largely on how willing you are to see meeting your aims as a team effort. The group you started with may need to develop into a team, but it may be that you need to be prepared to include others from your neighbourhood. As the word 'community' suggests, in order to express what God has in mind for your community, you need some kind of area, region, town, village, neighbourhood, people, population, sharing, or a sense of togetherness, in which or with which to make it happen. It is impossible to do it alone. They have already been involved in connecting with the issues. So when it comes to finding ideas about what to do within your community you probably won't be surprised that many of the answers will come from within your community itself, as will many of the resources which will make these ideas a reality. If you don't ask your community for input you may find yourself running dry. People in your community are your greatest resource, both for ideas and for action.

As you begin to consider the implications of growth through the process of Acting within Community, all sorts of questions about whether potential members have to be Christian or not in order to join your team will arise. It may well depend on the nature of the activity you are thinking of inviting them to join. Simple questions like, 'Will they feel comfortable with this?' or 'Do they agree with what we're doing?' may help you to make up your mind. Of course it is never that simple; whether they are comfortable or not may not be the issue. Believe it or not (and apologies if you're one of them), some groups or churches actually have policies on what level of faith people have to show before they are allowed to get involved. Sure, certain tasks may require some form of commitment to Christ, but is it really necessary for someone helping with the craft activities at the kids' club to have been baptised?

EXPRESS EXPERIENCE

Over 14 years of trying to develop some sort of model of integral mission, my personal view has changed dramatically. After starting with a rigid policy of refusing to allow non-Christians to join any of the teams I led, I eventually realised that what I was promoting was preventing what God was trying to achieve: gently using opportunities to connect people into his kingdom. People kept asking to help out and I kept refusing.

Jesus worked with all kinds of people regardless of their age, sex, political position, economic status, colour, creed, race or faith. Perhaps as his followers we need to do the same. People need to belong to something first, or at least feel welcomed, before they will even consider whether they want to believe or not. I am not suggesting you should adopt a policy of Together Anyone Achieves More: that's not TEAM, it's TAAM! They have to be right for the role, the task, the purpose, or at least you need to see they have the potential to be, in the same way Jesus did. Of course it is necessary to get all the appropriate police checks and references, but as far as their faith is concerned, mustard seed or towering oak, should it really matter? Which one of the disciples was a Christian when Jesus chose him for his team?

Ultimately this question is one for you, your group, and perhaps even the leaders to whom you are accountable, to consider, but seeing Christians and non-Christians working together for a common cause has been one of the greatest blessings I have had the privilege of witnessing in my short life as a Christian, a youth worker, a leader and a member of a community. Surely this is the aim of integral mission and what the Express Community process has been all about?

GROWING COMMUNITY

In 2 Kings 4:3-6 we find a widow not afraid of asking for help from her community when her family are in need. Her family's resources are limited and in order to be truly blessed she needs others to get involved: it is a team effort. As she scours her village looking for vessels to carry God's oil of blessing, her priority is not what they had been used for before, where they came from, how old they are or what colour they are, but their ability to make themselves available to be used.

God can use all things for his good purposes, but without empty vessels he can do nothing: see what he did to water and a few empty jars at Cana (Jn. 2:1-11). You may find willing people are the best resources you have.

Limiting your resources to those of your existing team may limit God's capacity to use you. When the vessels ran out the oil stopped flowing (2 Kgs. 4:6). Your ability to express effective community will be determined by how good you are at spotting the empty vessels God wants to use, those people who are prepared to empty themselves on behalf of others, which is what Isaiah 58:10 describes as God's desire for all his people. To be spent means to be able to lay aside your agenda in order to give everything to God's. The very nature of your community will mean many of the vessels you choose to use, or who choose you, will be broken and cracked through years of misuse or abuse. Here are a few tips for growing team:

Discover why people don't want to get involved. Are they afraid of volunteering? Have they been let down in the past? Are they apathetic? What might change this? Are they afraid of being a model to someone else or do they need to know they will have a model to follow and learn from? Are they afraid their insecurities might be exposed?

Discern whether this is someone who loves Jesus, loves people, loves his church and, most important of all, someone who loves the community. This will always be an area of potential compromise. Some activities you perform as a Christian group will be alien to someone without such a faith. The key is to be sensitive without losing identity.

Deploy them immediately. Take the initiative to get them involved. Speak to them whilst they seem excited by the prospect: don't let them go off the boil. Share your vision, aims and objectives and how you feel they might fit in and bring benefits. Ask for feedback, for their view of the situation. Suggest a fixed term for them to get involved, a way in and a way out if they need it. Promise support.

Develop people. Spend time with them, formally and informally. Offer training and encourage learning by doing. Sort out problems, concerns or grievances when they happen. Invest in emerging leaders; give them opportunities to flex their wings. The following checklist will help you in considering an individual's suitability for your team.

TEAM TICK LIST

1. Does this person have the actual or potential skill for the task?
   ☐ YES   ☐ NO

2. Is he or she motivated to seek excellence?
   ☐ YES   ☐ NO

3. Is he or she flexible enough to work with others?
   ☐ YES   ☐ NO

4. Will they complement the rest of the team?
   ☐ YES   ☐ NO

5. Have they a sense of humour and a tolerance of others?
   ☐ YES   ☐ NO

6. Are they willing to serve in any capacity that might be required?
   ☐ YES   ☐ NO

7. Will they develop a sense of *group* responsibility?
   ☐ YES   ☐ NO

8. Do they have a realistic appreciation of their strengths and weaknesses?
   ☐ YES   ☐ NO

9. Do they have the respect of those who know them?
   ☐ YES   ☐ NO

10. Would the team help them develop their gifts and abilities?
    ☐ YES   ☐ NO

GROWING PARTNERSHIPS

There is strength in working together. Get it right and you will feel both supported and surprised as you seek to act within community. Don't try to be self-sufficient within your team. Whatever ideas you choose to use to express community you will still find roles that can't be filled by the people you have already. Teamwork is therefore essential. A considerable amount of this chapter has focused on how you develop, maintain and possibly grow your own team. As we have begun to move on to consider how community itself may hold the key to your ability to express community, it is important not to rule out ideas that mean you are adding something to an existing group rather than taking something away to use in your own project. You may find yourself being called to join an existing team that is already working within your community. You may or may not be the leader of that team, in which case your role will be different, but the principles of what makes team work remain.

Express Community is about engaging people and their lives in order to create lasting change (for the better). Working with other agencies seeking to meet the same needs you have identified as key to your community is just as suitable a conclusion to reach from this Express Community process as forming your own team to do a different task. Don't rule anything out! Working in partnership with other agencies won't be easy: sometimes it will mean compromise or greater complications but most of the time it will provide confidence and increased capacity. It may mean having faith in the most unlikely people; sometimes it will mean being let down by the most unlikely people. Though your mission should not change, your priorities might. Your agenda may have to be put on the back burner for a while whilst you deal with someone else's pet project. The mission, aims, objectives and activities you will complete during Stage Three are there as a means of refocusing your attention; they will act as a reminder of what you are doing and who for. That's why it is important that you have them!

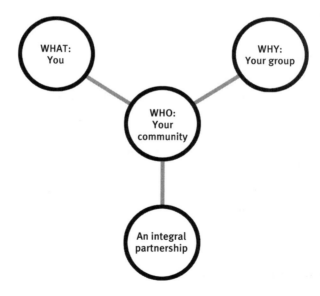

KEY QUESTIONS:

As a team leader how ready are you to do the following?

Encourage contribution from everyone – the loud and the quiet, the confident and the shy. Seek to build a sense of togetherness. Any decisions should be based on listening to information about the situation. Good communication is key. Meet as often as you can; talk as often as you can. Regular meetings, which are open and honest, will allow people to feel that their voice is being heard and their views are significant. It will also help to avoid undue overlap of activities and time wasting. Fostering relationships outside the group context are also important. Include socials, away-days or weekends away that are purely about you and your team and not just about what you have to do.

Enthuse, inspire and excite people. Enthusiasm comes from the Greek *entheisos*, which means 'God inside'. The 'feel' of a team matters. It is also important not to be afraid to celebrate success. Shake off the reserve some of us have towards achievement. At the same time, be realistic: be honest about mistakes and allow failure. It is important to be sensitive to conflicts.

Empower and affirm people. Release them and allow them to grow. Try and bring out the best in individuals and the team. Each member needs to be aware of his or her own responsibility, what they have to do and don't have to do. Consider Jesus' 'Disciple Cycle' as a way to build individuals and therefore the team.

Emphasise the values of what you are about, where you are heading and why. (This is particularly important for new people who are joining and may not have gone through the process that the original core team did.) Remember that your strategy is there to guide you and to remind you why you became a team in the first place. It should help you to avoid self-focusing, the pitfall of too much team-building. You may find you get on great as a group, so great that you never actually get out and get anything done! The key to an effective team is to maintain a balanced view of why you exist together. Remember that individuals matter, the whole team matters and the task matters.

Engage with God on a regular basis and encourage your team to do the same. Remember whose work you are doing! Pray for one another continually, as well as the issues. Seek intimacy with God as a group regularly and encourage individuals to build structures in their own life that enable this to happen naturally.

ENGAGE YOUR GROUP

How you choose to run this session will depend on how you have chosen to work through Stage Three: Acting within Community. It may be that this is Day Two of two, or the second half of a whole day focusing on action. The schedule opposite may help you plan your time (see Engage your group in Chapter 5 for details of how to plan the previous session).

OPTION A: TWO DAYS (SEPARATE OR A WEEKEND)
Day 2 of 2

Session 14:	09.30 – 10.30
Part A:	10.30 – 11.00
Break	
Part B:	11.30 – 12.00
Part C:	12.30 – 13.00
Lunch	
Express together:	13.30 – 14.00

OPTION B: ONE DAY (AFTERNOON SESSION)

Session 14:	13.30 – 14.30
Part A:	14.30 – 15.00
Break	
Part B:	15.30 – 16.00
Part C:	16.00 – 16.30
Express together:	16.30 – 17.00

Ideas

Stage Three: Session 14 is designed to help your group come up with two or three ideas of realistic responses to a key need in your community. These ideas may be to strengthen support of an existing initiative, to start a new initiative, or to affirm and support what individual group members are already doing.

Who is it for?

The workshop may be for your whole group, your church and in addition open to people in the wider community who have been involved in sharing their views, whether local residents or people with professional involvement in the area. Their presence at the workshop could be very useful in helping to test out ideas, and also helps to encourage partnership between Christians and the wider community. It will be up to you who you decide should be invited.

Key points

Ideas suggested need not be for just new initiatives. They could be as diverse as:

- providing more support to members of the group who through their contacts with family, neighbours and friends are already involved in meeting community needs
- affirming an existing group-run initiative and looking at ways of increasing its effectiveness
- expanding and developing an existing group-run initiative to meet additional needs identified
- beginning a new initiative to address an identified area of community need
- developing stronger links with an already established community initiative in the area, and channelling individuals and resources from the group into it
- entering into partnership with another group or community body to begin a new initiative

SESSION 14

IDEAS

YOU WILL NEED:

large sheets of paper, pens and paper

Having established your situation, mission and aims, the next question you will have to ask yourself is what you need to do in order to meet your aims. Most important of all, you need ideas. You'll have to help your group to hear about and learn from other groups involved in their communities. The session should give you a few innovative ideas for group involvement in the community but more importantly draw out some key principles of community involvement. It should help to stimulate the group to creative and innovative ideas of their own, appropriate to their own community, helping them see that small can be beautiful. This session provides brief snapshots of some innovative community development models. It will help you to think through appropriate responses to some of the issues in your own community.

Looking at the case-studies (10 mins)

Prior to the activity, stick each case-study on the walls of the room. (See Express together at the end of this chapter).

Ask people to wander around, read the case-studies, and jot down on a piece of paper:

1. How they feel on reading the various case-studies: excited? inadequate? hopeful? unmoved? etc.

2. What they think they can learn from the case-studies.

Feedback (20 mins)

Ask people to feed back on how they felt. Explore why people felt the way they did. You may want to point out that there is nothing unusual about these groups. Some of the groups are relatively small, with 20 or fewer members, so people should not feel intimidated.

Ask the group what they feel should have been learnt as a group from the experience of each of these groups.

If the discussion needs further impetus, you may find the following questions helpful:

- What do you think are the keys to making each initiative successful?
- What do the various groups have in common?
- In what ways do they relate to the community?
- How do they make use of their existing skills and resources?

The sort of points you may want to draw out of the discussions will stress the importance of:

- identifying what the needs are before jumping in and doing something
- working with the community in identifying the needs
- building relationships with those you are trying to help
- not being afraid to try out simple ideas
- being culturally sensitive
- making the most of existing skills and resources
- involving the local community in helping out in the initiative
- tackling the root causes of the problems

Write down on a large sheet of paper the points that the group comes up with. Ask the group what other principles they think are important in planning a community initiative.

Action planning (15 mins)

As people read what other groups have done, quite a few of the group are likely to get quite excited about what they themselves could do. You will want to tap into this enthusiasm. If your group is part of a church and the leadership have not taken part in this activity, you will need to consider how to present your ideas to them. You may wish to write a letter or organise a presentation, but there are other options. Alternatively, if the leadership have themselves participated in the activity, you may want to suggest they think through how best they communicate their ideas and learning to the wider church.

Conclusion (5 mins)

Sometimes we may feel overwhelmed at the task of getting involved in meeting the needs of our community. Indeed, many of the problems in our community are enormous, and offer no quick-fix solutions. However, as we have seen from some of the case-studies, groups can make a difference. The people of Israel returned from exile to see the temple lying in ruins. They despaired at the huge task ahead of them. For many, Zerubbabel's act of getting out his plumbline and beginning to make measurements for the new temple must have seemed like a bad joke. But as the angel of the Lord spoke to Zechariah, 'Who despises the day of small things?' (Zech. 4:10). Hopelessly inadequate though Zerubbabel's act seemed to be, from such small beginnings the temple was again rebuilt. From small beginnings, you too as a group can make a difference.

● ●

Activities (10 mins)

Return to your 'problem tree' and the groups you were in for the previous session. Add specific project ideas/activities to the end of your solutions.

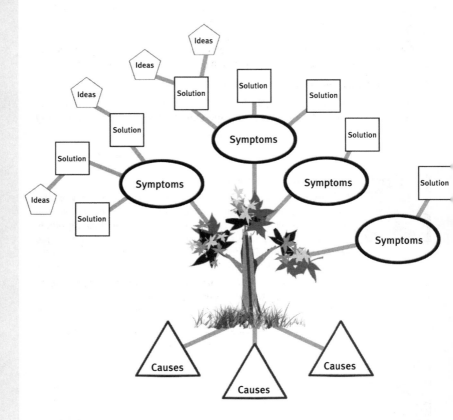

SESSION 14 (PART A)

OBJECTIVES (30 MINS)

YOU WILL NEED:

paper, pens and pencil

SWOT

You will find that no one idea you come up with will meet the need you have identified within your community and so it will be important to rank them in order of priority. Take each of the ideas in turn which you have identified as key to meeting your aims, and therefore the need, and using a sheet of A1 paper, begin to assess it by considering its:

- Strengths (what's good about)
- Weaknesses (what's bad about it)
- Opportunities (possible ways of implementing the idea)
- Threats (what may prevent you from using the idea)

Again consider whether it will:

- help you live out your mission as a group;
- meet the needs identified;
- benefit those most in need;
- get the community involved;
- be realistic in terms of its demands on group members' time, energy and resources.

For example, what are the strengths of running a youth café and what are the weaknesses? Are there any opportunities? Could you use the local church as a venue? What about threats? It will take a number of committed volunteers.

This simple exercise will cause you to dismiss some of the ideas as well as hopefully realising that some of these ideas might contribute to your aims. It will help you realise what needs to happen in order to make ideas work and in turn meet your aims.

● ●

BEEM

The next stage is to do a BEEM. Take a second sheet of A1 paper, place it directly against the SWOT sheet and Build, Eliminate, Exploit and Minimise some of the thoughts you came up with earlier. How can you *build* on your strengths? What about the weaknesses: how can you *eliminate* them? How do you *exploit* certain opportunities? For example, if you have identified the church hall as a possible venue for your event, you may feel you need to talk to the caretaker about the possibility of using it before it gets booked up. Finally, how might *you minimise* potential threats to your idea? For example, you might decide you need to find six more volunteers or invest in a team-building away-day every six months.

Objectives

Having SWOTed and BEEMed your ideas, you should now be in a position to begin to set some objectives. Objectives are designed to break your aim(s) down into smaller achievable tasks. They are short-term targets, which are usually set no more than two years in advance, which will enable you to achieve your aim(s). You will need to set a small number of broad objectives for the following months/years. These may refer to the numbers involved in your chosen activity, or the launch/development of a particular project. Set detailed objectives for all of your work. When setting objectives it is important to be SMART:

- Specific: Objectives should specify what they want to achieve.
- Measurable: You should be able to measure whether you are meeting the objectives or not.
- Achievable: Are the objectives you set achievable and attainable?
- Realistic: Can you realistically achieve the objectives with the resources you have?
- Timed: When do you want to achieve the set objectives?

The statement 'We will get lots more volunteers' is not SMART. The statement 'We will increase the number of volunteers from 15 to 20 in the current financial year' is SMART. Sometimes setting objectives is guesswork. Even when you don't really know what is realistic or achievable, it is helpful to set a target to aim for. Setting clear and good objectives should help you when it comes to thinking about your tactics and action plans, as they will be about fulfilling your objectives. So go on, have a go.

Set some objectives. What do you plan to do in response to the needs you have identified? Don't be afraid to start small and then think bigger.

Examples might include:

- increasing the number of people on the team from eight to 12 over the next six months
- increasing the number of young people you are in contact with each week from 20 to 40
- developing relationships with single parents in the community from three to five people during this month
- to deliver 50 'welcome to our community' packs every week to the new estate recently built to house asylum-seekers

SESSION 14 (PART B)

TACTICS (30 MINS)

YOU WILL NEED:

paper, pens or pencils

Write up on a flipchart three separate headings:

1. Short term

2. Medium term

3. Long term

Depending on the number of ideas on your 'problem tree' and the size of the group, you should either:

● read out each idea and ask the group as a whole to allocate it a number according to its priority,

or

● ask each of the discussion groups to allocate numbers to the ideas on the tree in front of them.

Take feedback on all the short-term ideas and write these up on an OHP or flipchart. You may need to clarify some of the ideas so that everyone understands what is being suggested. The reason for this is that it is best to start with something small and achievable, and once having built confidence, you can then return to some of the bigger ideas in the second and third categories.

In small groups, ask people to select their top three ideas from the first category of ideas just articulated by the whole group. Again it will be helpful to ask yourself:

● Will the idea help us live out our mission as a group?

● Will the idea meet the needs identified?

● Will the idea benefit those most in need?

● Will the idea get the community involved?

● Is the idea realistic in terms of its demands on group members' time, energy and resources?

SESSION 14 (PART C)

ACTION PLANNING (30 MINS)

YOU WILL NEED:

paper, pens or pencils

This is now getting down to the very detailed level. This is where you may need to get your diary and calculators out as you answer the following questions:

● What resources do you need – e.g. money, time, skills or talents – and who might be able to help you to supply them?
● When is it going to be done (e.g. month, year, etc)?
● Who is going to do it?

For example:

What will happen?	When will it happen?	Where will it happen?	Who is responsible?	How will people find out about it?	What is the cost?
Leaders' Training Day	September and January	Village hall	Leaders Helpers	Phone calls Emails Newsletter	£? for food £? for the venue £? for transport
Family Fun Day	October and February	Local	Team leaders Promotional person	Newspapers	£? for venue £? for bouncy castle £? for PA system

EXPRESS TOGETHER
CASE STUDIES

TOY STORY

A group of Christians in London found that single mothers in their community were finding it difficult to get out and meet people and as a result were feeling very isolated. They also recognised that many were struggling to afford toys for their children.

They came up with a simple way of beginning to address these two issues:

Every two weeks, someone from the scheme drops in to see the mother and brings a range of toys with them. As with a library, the mother can return some toys and borrow others. During the visits, there is usually time to build relationships and, where appropriate, offer further support.

ELDERLY CARE

A church in south-west London uses its premises during the week as a drop-in centre. It provides an opportunity for elderly people, who can often feel isolated in a community, to come together, to relax and enjoy each other's company.

One thing that makes the church centre distinctive is the warm relationships. The elderly people appreciate the welcoming atmosphere, the fact that spiritual issues are not ignored (there is a daily time of prayer) and the fact that everything is done to make them feel at home. For example, most of the elderly are from the Afro-Caribbean community and so food and the activities are given a distinctly Caribbean flavour.

WORK STATION

A youth group from the Midlands recognised that one of the biggest problems in the area was education. When they dug deeper it became obvious that part of the difficulty was the struggle many young people had with homework. Poor housing conditions made studying in a quiet environment almost impossible and parents did not always have the educational background to be able to help their children.

Consequently, the group, with the support of local Christian teachers, has set up a homework club, to provide extra lessons and support to children and young people on a Saturday morning.

COMMUNITY SUBWAY PAINTING

A group of Christians in south London is tackling a badly graffitied subway in their area by enlisting the support of the local community. Many people had wanted something done for years, but it was the group that took on the role of catalyst, drawing in the local residents' association, nearby schools, the community art college, and the local DIY shop to get involved in repainting the subway. They were even able to get the youth who had been responsible for most of the graffiti in the first place to help redesign the subway's new look – spray-painted murals, shapes and numbers.

A project that had seemed huge became possible, and has helped to draw the community together. The group made many contacts and relationships with the wider community.

CREDIT'S DUE

Churches in Cleethorpes came together to do something about a local problem: homelessness. They discovered many homeless people caught in a trap. 'No fixed address' meant claiming housing benefit was difficult, and no money meant they could not afford the deposit to rent that would give them their fixed address.

The churches devised a loan scheme that guaranteed the landlord's deposit, so enabling the family/individual to move in. Once in, they could claim benefit to pay the rent themselves.

Discovering further needs, the churches now provide debt counselling and a furniture-recycling scheme that allows those moving into homes to obtain low-cost furniture. They are also asking landlords to set a level of rent closer to the level of housing benefit.

LUNCHTIME CLUB

A Manchester group is helping to run a lunchtime club for local school children, at the invitation of the head, after children talked about school bullying at the youth club.

For several weeks, the same group of 10 children meet for small group activities, such as arts and crafts, drama and games. The aim is to build positive relationships between the bullies and bullied, helping them to reflect upon their behaviour. Through it, many bullied children have grown in confidence and self-esteem and some of the bullies have learnt to work with others positively. The children have so appreciated the group's input that many now also attend other activities run by local Christians.

RECYCLING

A group of Christians in Wales recognised that a key need in their community was for employment opportunities. Alongside this, many poorer families found new clothing and furniture way too expensive.

It decided to set up a clothes recycling scheme, which very quickly grew to the point that they were able to employ a local person to supervise the project. The money that the scheme continued to generate was used to start a furniture recycling business, which not only provided low-cost furniture, but also provided training for local people in carpentry and restoration. On the back of this scheme, a third business was set up, repairing and selling bikes: again it employed local people and provided a valuable service to the community.

1 G. Gordon, *What If You Got Involved?* (Carlisle: Paternoster Press, 2003), pp. 76-77.

LIVING
WITHIN
COMMUNITY

'Run in such a way as to get the prize'

(1 Cor. 9:24).

THE FINAL SCENE:
LIVING WITHIN COMMUNITY

A good book on local integral mission, just like a good film or TV programme, must surely finish with a rousing conclusion, a grand finale designed to send you off into the sunset with vision to change the world forever. Well, either this is not a good book, or perhaps it's just realistic. Your final picture of local integral mission may have not turned out quite as you intended; it may even need retuning now and again. It will be hard work, and you must think long term, but get it right and it should run and run.

Nevertheless, as the final credits roll and everybody leaves to return to their everyday lives, there is still one last question that needs answering: What did you decide to go for in the end?

Did you choose to go for a one-off, billion dollar extravaganza with stars galore, a thriller designed to keep you on the edge of your seat not knowing what will happen next, a drama with the potential of one crisis after another, a fly-on-the-wall documentary to look in on now and again but not get too involved in, or a serial soap with a walk-on part which you intend to play day in day out? Maybe it is best to 'finish' open-ended, not knowing what will happen next, in the hope that you will tune in the next day? Don't panic! Before you reach for the remote, there are currently no plans for a sequel to this long- running saga. Neither will there be a prequel, so no need to return to the debate on the value of evangelism as against social action and how to get the balance right. *Express Community* should have helped you to put to death that 'old has-been' in preference for a more integral view of mission within community, which involves 'just' living. The purpose of this conclusion is to ensure you don't find yourself waking up in the shower one morning suddenly realising that the Express Community process was all a dream and you're not actually Living within Community in the way you thought you were. So as you prepare to begin living differently, the following seven tips may give you something to think about over the next week. Follow them and they should help you continue to stay fresh and ready to respond to the new challenge of Living within Community ...

1. CUTTING THE TAPE

Tape is used for all sorts of occasions: patching things together which are broken, wrapping new gifts to give to someone you love, recording something crucial on TV that you don't want to miss and of course to mark an occasion when something new begins, such as a kind of opening ceremony. In many ways as you finish *Express Community*, it could be all of these things, but perhaps most significantly you are actually on the verge of deciding whether to open a chapter of your life and maybe that of your community. Rather than turning off and forgetting all the principles you have developed during this process, what you should be doing as you approach the end is placing yourself on standby for what you hope will be a more Christian way of Living within Community.

It will take time before you see that first fruit and there will be a lot of hard knocks and bruises along the way. However, providing you assess continually what you are doing and whether it is in line with the original vision God laid on your heart all those months ago, you should be okay. If you were a sprinter, your sports coach might advise you to 'never slow down, even when you think you can see the finish in sight; don't stop running, look neither to the left or to the right and run right through it … and don't forget to dip at the line!' Run right through the tape is sound advice. In a modern context, the tape is now a line or camera's eye, but the idea is the same: you cannot afford to stop, you have to keep going. The bad news (or maybe good news?) is that the finish may never come in your lifetime. However, providing you set yourself realistic aims and objectives, hopefully there will be plenty of short sprints to run which will keep you encouraged and provide some sense of achievement for you and your group.

Those old enough may remember the dreaded beep test at school. You start at one end of a hall or gym and the machine beeps, you then have only so many seconds to get to the other end before the machine beeps again. Nobody ever knows how long you've got; all you do know is that after the first beep sounds, the gaps between the beeps get shorter and shorter. Eventually people begin to drop out through sheer exhaustion, or they just can't make it to the other side of the hall before the next beeps sounds. Imagine for a moment you were to put two world-class athletes in that hall, one a sprinter and one a long-distance runner. You remove the beep but ask them to race each other by running from one wall to the next. Something deep inside the sprinter will mean he or she will burst out of the blocks and run as fast as he or she can for as long as they can, but the long-distance runner will probably pace themselves, jogging rather than sprinting. They'll last a lot longer, that's for sure. The point is that though you may be in a race, you're not being judged on how fast you complete it but by the fact that you are prepared to compete.

Living within Community is not a beep test: you don't get eliminated if you can't keep up, neither should you drop out through exhaustion. Provided you pace yourself, invest in creating a strong team who will share the burden and remain focused on the task, you should get the job done and you'll do it well. In 1 Corinthians 9:24-27 Paul offers some sound advice to any would be athlete: run for the prize, train hard, aim for the finish and most importantly follow the rules. There are no short cuts, so don't cheat.

2. COMMITTING TO TRAINING

Hebrews 12:1-2 provides Jesus as the ultimate example of someone with commitment. Of course his race meant that he had to endure the cross. It will take great sacrifice and self-denial to win the prize for your community. In both Romans 8:17-19 and 2 Corinthians 4:17-18 Paul says that, although it may be hard now, the prize is great and it will seem like nothing once we reach it – this from a man who suffered more than most for his calling. Of course he is talking about the kingdom of heaven, which may well be the prize for some in your community, but it could just as well be referring to the kingdom of heaven here on earth that should be your aim for your community.

1 Timothy 4:7-8 is key to an understanding of training. Physical exercise is beneficial but what is really required is a desire to train yourself to be godly, to practise those things that we would class as godly values. Once more we are back to Chapters 1 and 2, to the Beatitudes, to values like justice, mercy and humility. We're also talking about spending time in God's presence, learning from his example, being trained in his ways, and moving at his direction.

3. COMPLETELY FOCUSED

In Philippians 3:10-14 Paul declares that despite all his achievements, he didn't consider himself to have 'obtained it' or 'taken hold of it'. In his words, as far as he was concerned, his aim was to 'press on to take hold of that for which Christ took hold of me'. Whatever he may have achieved in the past was just that: past. What mattered most to him was the present and the future. Paul was not a man for resting on his laurels. Laurels of course were a circle of leaves, which were worn on the head of an important person or the winner of a competition.

There was a story on the news reporting on a team's preparation for the next Olympics. In the background you could see a number of men engaging in altitude training, trudging through thick snow with backpacks on. It was particularly crucial because the team for the Olympics had yet to be picked, and even though one of those trudging was a three-times Olympic rowing champion, he was not getting any preferential treatment. He had to go through all the same training, all the same selection processes, if he wanted to row again. The coach, in replying to a question as to why this was the case, simply replied, 'What's past is past.' He may have achieved great things but it doesn't give him the right to sit this one out and get in automatically. Whatever you do 'achieve' in your community, remember not to rest on your laurels but to press on towards that for which Christ has taken hold of you. Of course, the same can be said for failures: the past is irrelevant. It does not matter what you have done in the past; what matters is what is and what is to come.

4. CONSULTING THE RULEBOOK

Throughout this process, we have actively encouraged you to use *Express Community* not as a rulebook but as a guide, recognising the need to adapt it to make it work for you in your context. The same cannot be said of God's ultimate rulebook, the Bible. It is vitally important that whatever you choose to do within your community that it is done in exact accordance to God's will for his kingdom as revealed in his word. 2 Timothy 2:3-7 states that whatever a person's effort might achieve, he or she will not 'receive the victor's crown unless he competes according to the rules'.

There was a classic case of short-lived jubilation a few years ago, again at the Olympics, this time in Seoul in 1988. A Canadian sprinter won the 100 metres and at the same time broke the world record. It was an absolutely fantastic race; he literally left the rest standing. The hype and emotion that followed was incredible, but it was nothing compared to the depth of despair that he and the world felt when he failed a random drugs test and was found to be cheating. The race will go down in history, but for all the wrong reasons. The really sad thing was that he probably trained just like all the rest, hurt just like all the rest, but then cheated and got disqualified. There is a lot of pressure to succeed; it will come from all sorts of places, but in it all it is crucial that you stay loyal to your call and to your God. Revisiting *Express Community* will help you to recall the results of your community connection. It will help you rediscover your strategy if you feel you have lost your way. It will even help you to re-evaluate your life within community every now and again. But there is no substitute for spending time with God – reading his word, reflecting in prayer and relying on his Spirit.

5. CONTINUED DEVOTION

Continually devote yourself to prayer, as Paul says in Colossians 4:2, and at the same time, be prepared to hold yourself accountable to those in authority. Even Paul with all his achievements was never content to assume that his way was the right way. In Galatians 2:1-12 he shares that, 'I went in response to a revelation and set before them the gospel that I preach among the Gentiles. But I did this privately to those who seemed to be leaders, for fear I was running or had run my race in vain.' Paul had 14 years of successful ministry under his belt and yet he was prepared humbly to submit to those in authority and ask them whether what he was doing was appropriate. As leader you need to find people whom you can do that with. There have been too many occasions where people have begun a good work in the community and have gone astray on a power trip. In addition, as leader you too must be prepared to be available for your group as they seek someone to whom they can be held accountable. Of course, evaluation of anything you do, whether as a group, community, or with an objective observer, is key if you are to grow, develop and progress, which is why we have included one as part of this conclusion.

6. COMPLETE THE RACE

There are some wonderful examples that illustrate the value of completing the race, but the one that springs to mind is a classic Aesop fable – the story of the hare and the tortoise. The hare tears off but eventually begins to relax thinking the race is won. Whilst the hare sleeps, the tortoise takes over and wins the race. The moral of the story? Keep your mind on a job until it is finished. Slow and steady wins the race. To be effective in your life in community it is important that you and your group:

- create time to spend with God, both as individuals and as a group
- are clear about who you are and what God is calling you to do
- ensure you don't try to do everything and end up doing nothing
- take things steady, not being lazy, but plodding with purpose

Keep going until the task is finished or at least until you have someone in your sights. Let them have your baton, lead by example, leave them with a vision, lend them the book!

7. A CLOSING COMMENT ON COMMITMENT

If nothing else, *Express Community* should have made you realise that as Christians we are called to a greater commitment in following Christ and the daily example his life of integral mission set us. But what was his example? Jesus could have stopped at God's great 'co-mission', that is, with loving God and loving others, but he didn't. His life and death demonstrated that if you love God and you love others as the great co-mission suggests, you should go to any lengths to prove it. Jesus did.

> *This is how we know what love is: Jesus Christ laid down his life for us. And we ought to lay down our lives for our brothers (1 Jn. 3:16).*

He gave his whole life, and for that matter he died too, to demonstrate the extent to which he loved you, your team, your community and everybody's God, his Father (Jn. 3:16). Are you? Are you prepared to lay aside your life for the sake of others, putting them first and you last? That's the question you should take with you as you leave this book behind and the process of Express Community along with it. What are you left with? As a result of Reflecting within Community, Connecting within Community and Acting within Community, are you going to do everything in your own and God's power to ensure you keep Living within Community?

From what we have discovered throughout this journey, it seems that this is how to live a life worthy of God's calling (Eph. 4:1). *Express Community* has been all about integral mission, which in turn is all about Living within Community. Choosing to involve yourself in people's daily lives will ultimately involve the choices you make about your life each day: *who* you are, *what* you do and *why*. And ultimately the *why* determines the *how*! Your answers to these questions, developed throughout this Express Community process, determine how your developing picture of integral mission will look as you begin to commit to Living within Community. The process you have spent the last few months developing should help to inform the way you live the rest of your life. Make a commitment never to stop reflecting, connecting, acting and living within community. Use the answers to the *what*, *why* and *who* of community to inform *how* you choose to live your daily life in community.

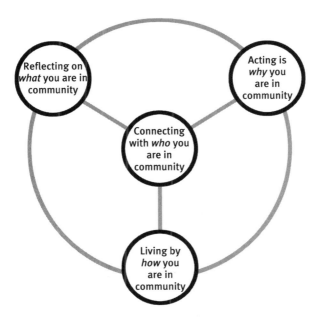

Live this way and you'll soon discover that you are:

Bringing local integral mission to life!

ENGAGE YOUR GROUP
EASY-TO-USE SESSION PLAN

SESSION 15

EVALUATION

Aim: To encourage the group regularly to check and reflect on its aims and objectives. To offer a model of a way to evaluate, monitor and assess progress.

YOU WILL NEED:

cardboard cut-out hands, paper, pens or pencils

Prior to this session you will need to ask your group to come with ideas about their hits, misses and maybes over the past several months.

If the 'work' undertaken as a result of *Express Community* is to continue, it is important that you constantly check and reflect on it by referring back to your aims and objectives. Your group should meet regularly to monitor and assess your progress. When you do, ask yourself whether:

- the activities you have set are being carried out on time
- you are still on track to achieve your objectives
- there are any problems you need to tackle
- you need any shift of emphasis
- you are overstretching yourselves
- you need more resources

Hits, misses or maybes? (30 mins)

There will always be setbacks and disappointments on any journey so when targets are not achieved within the agreed timetable, see it as part of a learning curve and ask the following questions. Encourage people to come to the evaluation session with what they consider to be the:

Hits   Misses   Maybes

Encourage individuals to feed back their thoughts. Make it fun: hand each person in the group a cardboard cut-out of a hand and ask them to comment on whether they agree that this particular issue was a hit, miss or maybe. Consider:

- why you failed to hit your target
- what problems you ignored or underestimated
- in what ways the reasons for failure were inside or outside of your team's control
- in what ways the problems could have been foreseen
- how the problems might be overcome

Impact (30 mins)

It may help to record your discussions by using the table below. Comment on each of your objectives in turn. The centre column should be used to record where you imagined you'd be at this stage (the example here is for a six-month review, but you may choose three months). The final column is to record what you have actually achieved:

This year's objectives?	1/2 year split	Where you are at:
Objective #1	e.g. a team of 20 volunteers	e.g. a team of 25 volunteers
Objective #2	e.g. painted 6 houses in George street	e.g. painted 3 houses in George Street
Objective #3	e.g. fitted the new kitchen in the youth café	e.g. stripped the wood chip off the walls in the youth café

COMMENTS ON OBJECTIVES

It will then be useful to comment on each objective, for example:

Objective #1
(Encourage comments on how you've done and reasons why you have met or not met your targets.)

TOP THREE ACTIVITIES

For this section encourage people to feed back on current activities aimed at meeting the objectives, such as promotional activities, training and events.

Activity	Progress	Outcome	Possible Outcome
e.g. cleaning the park's play area	e.g. purchased a brush	e.g. nothing to show so far, apart from a few people interested in helping out	e.g. clean and tidy area for local kids to play in

SWOT/BEEM (30 mins)

Finally, for each objective or issue you have raised, you need to think about how to build on your strengths, eliminate your weaknesses, exploit your opportunities and minimise your threats.

SWOT	Objective # 1	BEEM
Strengths		Build
Weaknesses		Eliminate
Opportunities		Exploit
Threats		Minimise

As a result of this session your mission or aims should not change dramatically. However, your situation may have changed as a result of your activities over the past several months. Whether you have achieved a hit, a miss or a maybe, you may find that you have to adjust some of your objectives in order to meet your aims more successfully. Record what is happening in the next six months to help achieve your objectives:

This year's objectives	Where we're at	Actions
Objective #1		
Objective #2		
Objective #3		

EXPRESS COMMUNITY!

GO ON: WHAT ARE YOU WAITING FOR?

EXPRESS EXPERIENCE

Don't forget, whatever you decide to do as a result of *Express Community* you are not alone. The Express Community process continues long after you complete the book. For worksheets, the latest information on training events, conferences and resources, to let us know how you're doing or just to keep in touch:

- Connect to: www.expresscommunity.org
- Click: expresscommunity@tearfund.org
- Call: 0845 355 8355 (ROI: 00 44 845 355 8355)
- Contact: Express Community, Tearfund, 100 Church Road, Teddington, Middlesex TW11 8QE.

CHRISTIAN ACTION WITH THE WORLD'S POOR

Tearfund is an evangelical Christian relief and development agency working through local partners to bring help and hope to communities in need around the world. The purpose of Tearfund is to serve Jesus Christ by enabling those who share evangelical Christian beliefs to bring good news to the poor.

■ NETWORK

provides youth leaders with resources, support and advice on how to tackle issues of justice, poverty and integral mission with their groups. Network's FREE magazine, published three times a year, includes biblical reflection, in-depth articles, easy-to-use session plans and practical ways to express faith at local, national and global levels.

■ ACTIV1ST

is Tearfund's FREE bi-monthly magazine for 14-17 year olds.

■ UNCOVERED

is Tearfund's FREE termly magazine for students and young adults.

■ TRANSFORM

is Tearfund's short-term opportunities programme – your chance to work alongside Tearfund partners in the UK and overseas. Options include, **Transform...**

International: 2 weeks, 4-6 weeks, or 4 months (18+).

Yourselves: Tailor-made UK and overseas projects for groups (14+).

UK: 2 weeks working alongside inner city churches (16+).

Year Team: 2 days a week working for Tearfund, 2 days working for a placement church or community project in the UK and a day studying or working.

To find out more about Tearfund:
Visit: www.tearfund.org/youth
Email: enquiry@tearfund.org
Phone: (+44) 0845 355 8355
Write to: Tearfund, 100 Church Road, Teddington, Middlesex, TW11 8QE, England.

CLOSING CREDITS

Bowyer, P. and Harley-Mason, G., *Lift the Label Youth Leader Pack. God' s Word on Lifestyle Choice* (Teddington: CPAS and Tearfund, 2003)

Chalke, Steve, *Faithworks Unpacked 3* (Eastbourne: Kingsway, 2002)

Chester, T., *Justice, Mercy and Humility. Integral Mission and the Poor* (Carlisle: Paternoster, 2002)

DFID, *Making Globalisation Work for the World' s Poor. An Introduction to the UK Government' s White Paper on International Development* (London: Folio, 2000)

Garmonsway, G. N., *The Penguin Concise English Dictionary* (London: Bloomsbury Books, 1991)

Gordon, Graham, *What if I Got Involved? Taking a Stand Against Social Injustice* (Carlisle: Paternoster, 2003)

Hope, A., Timmel, S. and Hodzi, C., *Training for Transformation: A Handbook for Community Workers* (Zimbabwe: Mambo Press, 1984)

Huczynski, A. and Buchanan, D. *Organisational Behaviour: An Introductory Text*, 5th edn (Edinburgh: Pearson Education Ltd, 2004)

Kidner, Derek, *Ezra and Nehemiah* (Leicester: IVP, 1979)

Lucado, Max, *Just Like Jesus* (Nashville, TN: Word Publishing, 1998)

Manser, M. H., *The Hodder Dictionary of Biblical Bible Themes* (London: Hodder & Stoughton, 1988)

Marshall, I. H., Millard, H., Packer, J. I., and Wiseman D. J., *New Bible Dictionary* (Leicester: Inter-Varsity Press, 1996)

Raistrick, T., *Church Community and Change* (Teddington: Tearfund, 2000)

Wallis, J., *The Call to Conversion* (London: Harper & Row, 1981)

EXTRAS: SUPPORT AND RESOURCES

■ BUSINESS ADVICE

For advice on all aspects of running a business: www.dti.gov.uk/er
0845 600 9006

■ CHILD PROTECTION

Churches' Child Protection Advisory Service:
www.ccpas.co.uk
0845 1204550

The NSPCC. The National Society for the Prevention of Cruelty to Children is the UK's leading charity specialising in child protection and the prevention of cruelty to children. They have been directly involved in protecting children and campaigning on their behalf since 1884.
www.nspcc.org.uk

Opportunities for Safety Education (A guide to principles and practices for Childminders) by the Royal Society for the Prevention of Accidents.
www.rospa.co.uk

■ DATA PROTECTION

Information Commissioner.
www.dataprotection.gov.uk
01625 545 745

■ EMPLOYMENT ISSUES

Peacock, Alison, *The Project Worker: A Guide to Employing Staff in Church Projects* (London: Church Urban Fund, 2000). ISBN 1 903251 01 X
www.cuf.org.uk
020 7898 1647

Employment Relations. An online guide to hours of work, pay entitlement, employees' rights, etc.
Department of Trade and Industry
www.dti.gov.uk/er

Interactive guidance on the national minimum wage and maternity rights:
www.tiger.gov.uk

Employment Law Zone Northern Ireland
www.legal-island.com/zone.htm

For lots of information relating to the legalities of employing staff and managing volunteers in Scotland, contact the Scottish Council for Voluntary Organisations.
www.scvo.org.uk/information/management/people/index.html
enquiries@scvo.org.uk
0131 556 3882

■ EQUAL OPPORTUNITIES

For loads of information on Equal Opportunity issues:
Equality Direct
www.equalitydirect.org.uk
0845 600 3444

For helpful downloadable leaflets on how small firms can avoid unlawful race, sex, and disability discrimination practices:

Equal Opportunities Commission
www.eoc.org.uk (leaflets available for England, Wales and Scotland)
0845 601 5901

For very relevant information about fair employment legislation contact the Equality Commission for Northern Ireland: 02890 500600.

■ FINANCIAL MANAGEMENT

The Charity Commissioners for England and Wales provides guidance. They also publish a small and helpful A5 booklet, Internal Financial Controls for Charities.
www.charitycommission.gov.uk
0870 333 0123

The Scottish Council for Voluntary Organisations provides a useful overview of good financial management.
www.scvo.org.uk/information/finance
0131 556 3882

Financial Systems Authority:
www.fsa.gov.uk

■ FUNDING

S. Clarke, *The Complete Fundraising Handbook* (London: Directory of Social Change, 2001). ISBN: 1900360845;
Price: £16.95
www.dsc.org.uk
info@dsc.org.uk
020 7209 5151

M. Norton and M. Eastwood, *Writing Better Fund-raising Applications*, 2nd edn (London: Directory of Social Change, 2002) ISBN: 1903991099;
Price: £14.95

www.dsc.org.uk
info@dsc.org.uk
020 7209 5151

Grant Making Trusts Directory and CDRom(produced by the Charities Aid Foundation in association with Directory of Social Change)
info@dsc.org.uk
020 7209 5151

J. Smyth, *The Guide to UK Company Giving* (London: Directory of Social Change, 2002) ISBN: 1903991021; Price: £25.00
www.dsc.org.uk
info@dsc.org.uk
020 7209 5151

Gweini Network email service (Wales focused):
Contact: Dan Boucher
gweini@freeuk.com

For free software programmes that help you draw up grant applications and budgets:www.funderfinder.org.uk

Scottish Churches Community Trust:
admin@scct.org.uk
0141 336 3766

'Funding for Voluntary Action' A free booklet that lists local grant making trusts for Northern Ireland. For more information contact the Community Fund for Northern Ireland at Community House, City Link Business Park, 6A Albert Street, BT12 4HQ.

■ FUNDING WEBSITES

A website about government funding, which pulls together information about most government grants for the voluntary sector:
www.volcomgrants.gov.uk

A trust-funding database published by the Directory of Social Change:
www.trustfunding.org.uk

Access Funds. Information on sources of funding for the British non-profit sector: www.access-funds.co.uk

BT Community Connections. A UK-wide awards scheme to enable local community projects. Awards of internet-ready computers are made to individuals or groups who wish to make a positive impact in their community. There is an online application form
www.btcommunityconnections.com

The Esmée Fairbairn Charitable Trust makes grants in five sectors: arts and heritage, education, environment, social and economic research, and social welfare: www.efct.org.uk

Grants Online. Information on sources of funding for the British non-profit sector: www.grantsonline.org.uk

Information on sources of funds for the British non-profit sector:
www.j4b.co.uk

Lloyds TSB Foundation
An application form can be downloaded from the website, which also has application guidelines.
www.lloydstsbfoundations.org.uk

New Opportunities Fund:
www.nof.org.uk

Directory of Social Change. Information about smaller grants is now available online, as well as information about printed guides.
www.dsc.org.uk

ACF. Gives details of members of the Association of Charitable Foundations. www.acf.org.uk

A website about government funding, which pulls together information about most government grants for the voluntary sector: www.volcomgrants.gov.uk

Trust-funding database: www.trustfunding.org.uk

■ **HEALTH AND SAFETY**

Health and Safety Executive. All aspects of health and safety covered, including workplace issues. www.hse.gov.uk 0870 154 5500

■ **MONITORING AND REPORTING**

Charities Evaluation Service: www.ces-vol.org.uk 0207 713 5722

Community Development Foundation (England, Scotland and Wales): www.cdf.org.uk 0207 226 5375

Scottish Community Development Centre: www.scdc.org.uk 0141 248 1924

G. Whitting, *Developing Aims and Objectives* (London: Charities Evaluation Service, 1993). ISBN: 189796 025; Price £6.50 (a short and friendly A5 publication). www.ces-vol.org.uk enquiries@ces-vol.org.uk 020 7713 5722

A. Connor, *Monitoring Ourselves* (London: Charities Evaluation Service, 1999). ISBN: 1 897963 00 9; Price £7 (short and friendly A5 publication). www.ces-vol.org.uk enquiries@ces-vol.org.uk 020 7713 5722

■ **PROJECT MANAGEMENT**

Pay your local Council for Voluntary Service (CVS) a visit. Many groups setting up new initiatives have found their knowledge of the local area and advice on project management invaluable. To find out more about your local CVS, call the National Association of Councils for Voluntary Service (NACVS). www.nacvs.org.uk nacvs@nacvs.org.uk 0114 278 6636

Churches' Community Work Alliance Provides advice, support and resources to help church-related community work. www.ccwa.org.uk

Wired Up information bulletin: wiredup@tearfund.org 020 8943 7755

A. Davies, *Managing for a Change: How to run Community Development Projects*, 2nd edn (London: Intermediate Technology Publications, 1997). ISBN 1 95339 3991; Price £9.95.

Scottish Council for Voluntary Organisations: www.scvo.org.uk/essentials/default.htm

enquiries@scvo.org.uk
0131 556 3882 (Edinburgh)
0141 221 0030 (Glasgow Branch)
01463 235 633 (Inverness Branch)

Frontier Youth Trust Ireland provides advice, support and resources to help church-related community youth work.
www.fytireland.org
info@fytireland.org
02890 743354

■ VOLUNTEER MANAGEMENT

For information and resources for managing volunteers, including a full range of free and helpful fact sheets, contact Volunteering England.
www.volunteering.org.uk
020 7520 8900

For free information sheets on managing volunteers in Wales, contact the Welsh Council for Voluntary Action.
www.wcva.org.uk/working/index.html
02920 431700

Volunteer Development Scotland:
www.vds.org.uk
01786 479593

Volunteer Development Agency Northern Ireland:
www.volunteering-ni.org
02890 236100

Volunteer Development England:
www.vde.org.uk

Scottish Council for Voluntary Organisations.
www.scvo.org.uk/essentials/default.htm
enquiries@scvo.org.uk
0131 556 3882

YOUTHWORK
THE PARTNERSHIP

Oasis, the Salvation Army, Spring Harvest, Youth For Christ and Youthwork Magazine are working together to equip and resource the Church for effective youth work and ministry.

YOUTHWORK THE INITIATIVES

■ YOUTHWORK – THE CONFERENCE

An annual training conference to inspire, network and equip – managed by Spring Harvest. www.youthwork.co.uk/conference

■ YOUTHWORK – THE MAGAZINE

A monthly magazine providing ideas, resources and guidance – managed by CCP. www.youthwork.co.uk/magazine

■ YOUTHWORK – THE TRAINING

What Every Volunteer Youth Worker Should Know

A 9 two-hour session foundation course for busy 'extra-timers' who want to know the basics, and fast! – managed by Oasis Youth Action. www.youthwork.co.uk/training/volunteerscourse

The Art of Connecting

An eight-session/12-hour course for young people in 'three story' evangelism – managed by YfC. www.youthwork.co.uk/training/youngpeople

■ YOUTHWORK – THE WEBSITE

A gateway to online resources, community, information and learning – managed by Youthwork Magazine. www.youthwork.co.uk

■ **YOUTHWORK – THE RESOURCES**

A range of books and materials edited by Danny Brierley and John Buckeridge – managed by Spring Harvest Publishing, an imprint of Authentic Media.

To find out more about Youthwork the Resources:
Visit: www.youthwork.co.uk/resources

Going Deeper – theory, theology and practice.

Developing Practice – 'how to...' guides, methods and inspiration.

Resourcing Ministry – ready-to-use ideas.

YOUTHWORK THE PARTNERS

■ **OASIS YOUTH ACTION**
the youth division of Oasis Trust, empowers young people and equips youth workers.

■ **OASIS YOUTH PARTICIPATION**
empowers those aged 11 to 25 years

■ **OASIS PASSION**
Mobilises young people in social action.

■ **OASIS FRONTLINE TEAMS**
is a UK-based gap year programme.

■ **OASIS GLOBAL ACTION TEAMS**
place young adults in different countries.

■ **OASIS YOUTH WORK TRAINING**
equips youth workers and ministers

■ **OASIS WHAT EVERY VOLUNTEER YOUTH WORKER SHOULD KNOW**
is a 9 session/18 hour course for volunteers.

■ **OASIS YOUTH WORK DEGREE (BA HONS/DIPHE)**
is a professional training programme in youth work and ministry.

■ OASIS YOUTH ESTEEM

enables youth workers and church volunteers to support young people's personal, social and health education in their local schools.

■ OASIS YOUTH INCLUSION

tackles social exclusion among young people and children. It offers mentoring, group work and sexual health/relationship education.

To find out more about Oasis Youth Action:
Visit: www.OasisTrust.org/YouthAction
Email: YouthAction@OasisTrust.org
Phone: (+44) 020 7450 9044.
Write to: Oasis Youth Action, 115 Southwark Bridge Road,
London, SE1 0AX, England.

The Salvation Army for a new generation

ALOVE is The Salvation Army for a new generation. Launched in 2004, ALOVE is an expression of The Salvation Army within youth culture. ALOVE is calling a generation to dynamic faith, radical lifestyle, adventurous mission and a fight for justice. ALOVE provides young people and young adults with ongoing opportunities to engage in culturally relevant worship, cell and small group discipleship, innovative mission and world changing social action. ALOVE is creating personal development and training programmes to develop leaders and missionaries for the 21st Century. ALOVE is pioneering new expressions of church, youth work and social inclusion in communities around the United Kingdom and Ireland.

To find out more about ALOVE:
Visit: www.salvationarmy.org.uk/ALOVE
Email: ALOVE@salvationarmy.org.uk
Phone: + 44 (0) 20 8288 1202
Write to: ALOVE UK, The Salvation Army, 21 Crown Lane,
Morden, Surrey, SM4 5BY

Equipping the Church for action

Spring Harvest is an inter-denominational Christian organisation whose vision is to 'equip the Church for action'. Through a range of events, conferences, courses and resources they seek to enable Christians to impact their local communities and the wider world. Spring Harvest Holidays provide an opportunity in France for relaxation and refreshment of body, mind and spirit.

Their Main Event, held every Easter, attracts some 60,000 Christians of all ages, of which over 10,000 are young people. This event also includes specific streams which cater for over 2000 students. Alongside the teaching programme, Spring Harvest provide a range of resources for young people and those that work in youth ministry.

To find out more about Spring Harvest:
Visit: www.springharvest.org
Email: info@springharvest.org
Phone: (+44) 01825 769000
Write to: Spring Harvest, 14 Horsted Square, Uckfield,
East Sussex, TN22 1QG, England.

YFC, one of the most dynamic Christian organisations, are taking good news relevantly to every young person in Britain. They help tackle the big issues facing young people today. They're going out on the streets, into schools and communities and have changed the lives of countless people throughout the UK.

Their staff, trainees and volunteers currently reach over 50,000 young people each week and have over 50 centres in locations throughout the UK. They also provide creative arts and sports mission teams, a network of registered groups and a strong emphasis on '3 story' evangelism. YFC International works in 120 nations.

To find out more about YFC:
Visit: www.yfc.co.uk
Email: yfc@yfc.co.uk
Phone: (+44) 0121 550 8055
Write to: YFC, PO Box 5254, Halesowen,
West Midlands B63 3DG, England.

Youthwork Magazine is published monthly by CCP Limited. It is Britain's most widely read magazine resource for equipping and informing Christian youth workers. It provides ideas, resources and guidance for youth ministry. CCP also publish Christianity+Renewal, Christian Marketplace and Enough magazines. CCP is part of the Premier Media Group.

To find out more about Youthwork Magazine:
Visit: www.youthwork.co.uk
Email: youthwork@premier.org.uk
Phone: (+44) 01892 652364
Write to: Youthwork Magazine, CCP Limited, Broadway House,
The Broadway, Crowborough, TN6 1HQ, England.